Business Wat[...]
Understanding Bus[...]

For Alison and Jill who have a good head for business

Business Watching
Understanding Business Life

Adrian Furnham and Barrie Gunter

Whurr Publishers Ltd
London

First published in Great Britain by
ABRA Press
45 Thornhill Square, London N1 1BE

Reprinted 1996 by
Whurr Publishers Ltd
19b Compton Terrace, London N1 2UN, England

British Library Cataloguing-in-Publication Data
A catalogue record for this book is available from the
British Library.

ISBN 1-86156-023-0

Printed and bound in the UK by Athenaeum Press Ltd,
Gateshead, Tyne & Wear

CONTENTS

FOREWORD

A psychologist, it is said, is someone who goes to the *Folies Bergeres* to look at the audience. Whether they deserve or merit it, psychologists have a reputation for being observant and making perceptive, often counter-intuitive, remarks about everyday behaviour. For many of them, the everyday, the mundane, the ordinary is odd, extraordinary and worthy of explanation, while the abnormal and peculiar seems pretty usual and expected. It is the ability to challenge and explain the everyday thoughts and actions of people that makes psychology such an interesting subject.

The authors are academic occupational psychologists and management consultants. As part of our research we have to deal with a wide variety of corporate issues: how to select the best candidates; which performance management system to introduce; how to motivate disgruntled and alienated staff; how to devise a way to measure and then change corporate culture; whether to recommend various training courses; how to modify the physical working environment to maximize comfort; whether it is possible to detect honesty, integrity and dissimulation in employees; setting up businesses in foreign countries; and so on.

As part of this research we have to read the scholarly journals and books. But we also follow the 'thoughts' of the business gurus currently in favour, whose ideas, catch phrases and concepts have such a profound effect on the behaviour of people in business. And yet the most interesting part is actually collecting the data: observing, interviewing, and testing people at work. The power of organizations to mould behaviour and render employees actualized and satisfied, angry and depressed, brainless automata, egotistical megalomaniacs or helpless pawns in some high corporate chess game, is quite fascinating.

Work is clearly of fundamental importance to most adults. In the average day they may spend eight hours at work, eight at leisure and eight at sleep, but it is quite often the working hours that most influence and occupy them. This book is about the vicissitudes and ephemera of business life. It begins with two short tests which allow managers to assess, in a light-hearted way, the type of managers they are. These are followed by a collection of more than forty short essays on various aspects of behaviour at work. Each essay has been stimulated by some actual experience in the business world that has surprised, amazed, or puzzled us. Some of the topics are 'hot' in the sense that they are currently in fashion, while others are luke warm, but crucially important all the same. Some of the essays deal with the way business can or should be done in order to maximize effectiveness, results and success in different corporate contexts and situations.

We have tried after each essay to highlight some general learning points about the topic. They are meant to crystallize practical advice for astute business people, be they hard-pressed, stressed, or relaxed. This is neither a text book nor a heroic story of turning around a failing business. There are enough of those on the shelves.

We enjoyed writing the essays. In doing so they have helped us to make sense out of our experience and served to communicate it to others. Versions of some of the essays have appeared in business and financial papers and magazines, and have attracted critical interest. We have pulled them together in this book to explore, elucidate and expound upon a number of recurrent themes which managers and organizations regularly have to address. We don't pretend to have all the answers. This book is not the last word in best business practice. It does, however, attempt to draw attention to handy rules of thumb, or points to consider, designed to be of use to the purposeful manager or those who aspire to that position.

We have Lee Drew and Kate Bradford to thank for cheerfully word-processing and endlessly redrafting these essays with lightning efficiency, good humour, and chocolate biscuits.

Adrian Furnham
Barrie Gunter
London 1994

COMMON SENSE MANAGEMENT

Common sense, by definition, is supposed to be the mostly widely distributed quality in the world and nearly everybody believes they have a good measure of it. Many recruitors look for, and all managers are supposed to have, common sense. But what is common sense in the manager's world? And if management is common sense, why bother to teach it? In fact management science is seen by many as an oxymoron, akin to military intelligence, popular culture and low-cost lawyers.

The so-called 'discipline' of management science often has low status in business schools, partly because the hard men of figures despise the soft waffle of organizational behaviour. Management science is thought to be a trivial, expensive and pointless exercise in describing or proving what we already know. All findings are intuitive, unsurprising and uninformative; worse, it is packed with esoteric, mid-Atlantic jargon which obfuscates common sense in the pretence of clarifying it.

But there are serious problems with the common sense argument. first, common sense is frequently contradictory. 'Clothes make the man' is at odds with 'you can't make a silk purse out of a sow's ear'. 'Out-of-sight, out-of-mind' and 'absence makes the heart grow fonder' also seem contradictory. Although it is possible that both are true under different circumstances, common sense does not tell you which.

Secondly, if all management is common sense, nothing can be counter-intuitive or the result of faulty reasoning. Research in the sciences is full of such examples and it would not be surprising if some aspects of management science were the same; that is, the opposite of common sense.

It could be argued that current management knowledge is in fact absorbed from management science as it is frequently popularized in newspapers and magazines. Thus, ironically, common sense could be the result of the ideas of management science being commented upon in the popular press. A frequently-discussed finding from research cannot remain unknown to managers, any more than a joke can remain funny to people who hear it over and over again.

If all management is common sense and most people supposedly have this curious trait, why is there so much disagreement on management issues, processes and procedures?

When managers try to specify the 'competencies' essential for high-flyers in a company, many are tempted to include common sense, despite the fact that it is almost impossible to define, measure and therefore select. It may indeed be like the search for the Holy Grail-long-standing, complicated and unsuccessful. But why not test yourself? Are the following statements true or false? Mark them accordingly and see how you rate on the common sense factor.

---

1   If you pay someone for doing something they enjoy, they will come to like this task even more.   T ❑ F ❑

2   Most people prefer challenging jobs with a great deal of freedom and autonomy.   T ❑ F ❑

3   Most people are more concerned with the size of their own salary than with the salary of others.   T ❑ F ❑

4   In most cases, workers act in ways that are consistent with their attitudes.   T ❑ F ❑

5   In bargaining with others, it is usually best to start with a moderate offer, near to the one you desire.   T ❑ F ❑

6   In most cases leaders should stick to their decisions once they have made them, even if it appears they are wrong.   T ❑ F ❑

7   When people work together in groups and know their individual contributions can't be observed, each tends to put in less effort than when they work on the same task alone.   T ❑ F ❑

8   Even skilled interviewers are sometimes unable to avoid being influenced in their judgement by factors other than an applicant's qualifications.   T ❑ F ❑

9   Most managers are highly democratic in the way that they supervise their people.   T ❑ F ❑

10 Most people who work for the government are low risk-takers.   T ❑ F ❑

11 The best way to stop a malicious rumour at work is to present covering evidence against it.   T ❑ F ❑

12 As morale or satisfaction among employees increases in any organization, overall performance almost always rises.   T ❑ F ❑

13 Providing employees with specific goals often interferes with their performance: they resist being told what to do. T❑ F❑

14 In most organizations, the struggle for limited resources is a far more important cause of conflict than other factors such as interpersonal relations. T❑ F❑

15 In bargaining, the best strategy for maximizing long-term gains is seeking to defeat one's opponent. T❑ F❑

16 In general, groups make more accurate and less extreme decisions than individuals. T❑ F❑

17 Most individuals do their best work under conditions of high stress. T❑ F❑

18 Smokers take more days sick leave than do non-smokers. T❑ F❑

19 If you have to reprimand a worker for a misdeed, it is better to do so immediately after the mistake occurs. T❑ F❑

20 Highly cohesive groups are also highly productive. T❑ F❑

1-5 F❑   6-10 T❑   11-17 F❑   18-19 T❑   20 F❑

If you scored five or less, why not try early retirement? Scorers of six to twelve should perhaps consider an MBA. A score of sixteen or above, yes, indeed, you do have that most elusive of all qualities: common sense.

Einstein defined common sense as the collection of prejudices people have acquired by the age of eighteen, while Victor Hugo maintained that common sense was acquired in spite of, rather than because of, education. It might be a desirable thing to possess in the world of management, but don't kid yourself that it is very common. Perhaps a close reading of the rest of this book might help low scorers acquire a bit more common sense.

DIAGNOSING YOUR MANAGEMENT TYPES

A pessimist is an optimist who has had experience. Listen to the American management gurus, who seem to model both their delivery style and their beliefs on tele-evangelists, and you might believe that all workers are fundamentally good, diligent and legal. All that is required is a corporate vision, sincerity, and a caring, ethical boss and the workforce will deliver.

The optimist, it is said, believes that we live in the best of all possible worlds and the pessimist fears this is true. Is the pessimist one who, when he has the choice of two evils chooses both, or is he a realist? Is a pessimist one who feels bad when he feels good for fear he'll feel worse when he feels better, or simply a shrewd and accurate observer of life? The British seem more reserved and sceptical than other nationalities. More used to the threat of the stick than the promise of the carrot, they appear not to hold such a rosy view of their fellow man, and less still of their fellow woman.

Followers of the French idealist Rousseau stand in sharp contrast to the bleak perception of the Englishman Thomas Hobbes. The pessimistic manager might believe that 'man was born free but everywhere is in *trains*', on his way to a nasty, brutish, tedious and unsatisfying job.

For some, the experience of management is that people avoid work because they inherently dislike it. They have to be completely controlled, directed, bullied and threatened. They prefer not to show responsibility or empowerment and need to be constantly monitored.

About thirty years ago an American academic called McGregor, who was interested in what determined a person's leadership style, said that managers were likely to hold one of two 'philosophies' about workers. One, labelled THEORY X, maintained that people don't like work, avoid it, have little ambition, try to avoid responsibility and need firm direction, control and coercion. Subscribers to THEORY Y maintained that under the right conditions people not only work hard, showing commitment and talent, but also seek increased responsibility and challenge.

Test yourself to see if you are a Theory X or Y believer.

Give yourself:

4 for strongly agree,
3 for agree,
1 for disagree
0 for strongly disagree

YOUR ASSUMPTIONS ABOUT PEOPLE AT WORK

1 Almost everyone could probably improve his or her job performance quite a bit if he or she really wanted to.	4	3	1	0
2 It's unrealistic to expect people to show the same enthusiasm for their work as for their favourite leisure-time activities.	4	3	1	0
3 Even when given encouragement by the boss, very few people show the desire to improve themselves on the job.	4	3	1	0
4 If you give people enough money, they are less likely to worry about such intangibles as status or individual recognition.	4	3	1	0
5 Usually, when people talk about wanting more responsible jobs, they really mean they want more money and status.	4	3	1	0
6 Being tough with people will usually get them to do what you want.	4	3	1	0
7 Because most people don't like to make decisions on their own, it's hard to get them to assume responsibility.	4	3	1	0
8 A good way to get people to do more work is to crack down on them once in a while.	4	3	1	0
9 It weakens a person's prestige to admit that a subordinate has been right and he/she been wrong.	4	3	1	0
10 The most effective supervisor is one who gets the results management expects, regardless of the methods used in handling people.	4	3	1	0
11 It's too much to expect that people will try to do a good job without being prodded by the boss.	4	3	1	0
12 The boss who expects his or her people to set their own standards for superior performance will probably find they don't set them very high.	4	3	1	0
13 If people don't use much imagination or ingenuity on the job, it's probably because relatively few people have much of either.	4	3	1	0
14 One problem in asking for the ideas of subordinates is that their perspective is too limited for their suggestions to be of much practical value.	4	3	1	0
15 It's only human nature for people to try to do as little work as they can get away with.	4	3	1	0

Score under 20 and you are an optimist. You probably trust your subordinates and use a wide range of rewards. You may prefer group participation in decision-making and like people to be well informed.

Score 21 to 30 and we see more caution with substantial but not complete confidence and trust in subordinates. You wish to keep control of most major decisions.

Score 31 to 45 and some may consider you a benevolent autocrat. You have a rather condescending confidence and trust, such as a master has in a servant. You tend to believe in economic motives and don't fraternize with your staff.

Score 45 and above and, let's face it, you're a cynic about the average worker. High scorers may even be exploitative autocrats who have no confidence in their subordinates, preferring physical and economic security as a motivational force. All stick and no carrot.

Top scorers despise 'soft' management techniques and maintain that the Department of Hard Knocks at the University of Life taught them what they know. Low scorers recoil in horror at the monster they see in the high scorer, equally convinced that their experience at work tells them they are right. Neither side is prepared to concede.

Hence we need the understanding to know the things we cannot change about workers; the courage to change and improve the things we can change; and the wisdom to know the difference.

I
SELECTION

We begin by examining a number of general issues about selection and recruitment of individuals. It is both difficult and very important to select the good candidates and reject the bad candidates. In their desperation for subtle but valid measures, human resources experts have turned to the various methods mentioned in this section: *biodata*, or actual detailed biographical facts of a person's life; *psychological testing*, still the flavour of the month in some circles; even *astrology*. Most organizations call for *references* and *testimonials* which are also considered. But the standard *interview* is the most popular method. Some of the implications of odd questions such as 'what do you do in your spare time?' are considered in this section.

Selection is one of the most interesting aspects of business life. People hold strong beliefs about how it is best done, but often have little in the way of facts to back up their passionately held assertions!

A. References, Testimonials and Letters of Recommendation

Despite what we all know about their shortcomings, the employment interview and the reference letter of recommendation remain together the two most prevalent methods of evaluation used by prospective employers. Enough has been said and written about the employment interview, but what of the quaint and curious custom of requesting letters of reference and testimonials? Why do employers call for them? Are they at all useful or valid? How easy is it to spot classic lies, attempts to fudge or obfuscate?

Why does the practice of requiring letters of recommendation, called for in numbers roughly proportional to the status of the job, yet remain so prevalent? What employers are usually doing when they seek out references is to increase the size of the selection committee, adding to the number of people making judgements about the candidate, and spreading the blame or at least diffusing responsibility. Furthermore, reference writers are supposed to know the candidate extremely well and be in a position to comment on his or her behaviour, skills, health, abilities and temperament on, as well as off, the job. In this sense they have a potentially important role as a source of privileged information about a candidate. This input may be particularly significant given the difficulty of trying to get rid of people that one has mistakenly appointed, and the need to find out about anything that a candidate is trying to hide.

Requests for references come in many forms, as indeed do testimonials, though we are probably seeing less of the latter these days. Some simply tell the referee that a person known to them (and presumably nominated by them) has applied for a certain position and would they be so kind as to state the extent to which they felt the candidate is suitable. Other requests require comment on a range of features of job-related behaviour of candidates, such as the extent to which they are punctual, socially adept, computer-literate and prone to taking uncertificated sick leave. More commonly, thanks to marketing mentality, some references invite the source to fill out rating scales going from 'outstanding' to 'poor' and using those wonderfully school-masterly phrases such as 'satisfactory' and 'average'. These instruments resemble those never-completed questionnaires found in various hotel chains that boast complete homogeneity of decor and cuisine irrespective of the country in which they are located. And, of course, they include a stamped addressed envelope to encourage compliance.

The range, format and purpose of references never cease to amuse. An interesting illustration of reference-requesting carried to an extreme concerned a student of one of the authors who applied once for a holiday job at Harrods. For some reason it was thought she would be well-suited to the fish counter. The reference request duly arrived and was dutifully completed as required. Of course, it was never mentioned that she was the sickly type, given to taking to her bed when the trials and tribulations of this fleeting world got too much for her. Neither was it disclosed that she was a vulgar Marxist, opposed to nearly everything that the citadel of capitalism in Knightsbridge stood for. In fact, it was rather a difficult task knowing what to write ... 'Miss Patterson has dab hand with a halibut' ... 'She can even sell gravadlax to the Scandinavians' ... 'She is an expert on flat fish, especially gutting the turbot'. Quite why the store required two references for just four weeks work is a puzzle.

More recently, some reference requests have taken on the form of a four-page questionnaire that seems more exhaustive than is required for positive vetting! It could be a way of collecting what is now called biodata and takes hours to complete. This type of selection procedure is dealt with in the next section. Furthermore, what about the legal status of such documents? Do referees' observations, estimates and ratings count in evidence against the candidate? There are three factors which render references of whichever sort pretty worthless: first, referees are frequently chosen or nominated by the candidates and so are likely to be biased; secondly, there are unwritten, implicit and hence ambiguous rules for writing references in code; and thirdly, an interviewer cannot be sure of the motives of the referee in completing the reference request. The first problem lies in the nature of the source from whom the references are obtained. Some interview panels are completely non-specific, requesting letters from 'two people who know you well'. Others specify your boss, immediate superior, former lecturer ... but these often give the candidate pretty extensive leeway to choose another alternative. For instance, if a candidate suspects that the person directly above them will not write a good (possibly dishonest) reference, they may simply go up the ladder or along the organizational chart to find somebody who will. It is comparatively rare that candidates are required to get a reference from someone mentioned by name, and hence the exact choice of reference writer is open to potential abuse.

One trick is to get a high status referee. One student of the first author from an old Commonwealth country had applied to his college and nominated as referees the Prime Minister and the Lord Chief Justice of his homeland! Another student from an Asian kingdom nominated the king as referee and under 'Occupation of Father' on her form was Crown Prince. Just a hint of corruption there, or at least an attempt to impress.

Thus, because candidates seek out people who are likely to write good, socially desirable references for them, rather than those who perhaps should write the reference, know them well or are at least likely to write the truth, references are a potential source of inaccurate details about job applicants.

The fact that references are written in a sort of code of their own makes them difficult to crack. References are a bit like low church funeral eulogies in that they may contain only praise. They can be dreadfully one-sided and it is, on occasions, quite difficult to recognise either the dearly departed or the refereed, however well one knew them. Some nationalities are worse than others: they write as if every student is an Einstein, every worker a Stakanovite, every leader a Churchill. These references are completely worthless because they fail completely to discriminate the able from the unable, the competent from the incompetent, the efficient from the inefficient.

The British, however, are uncomfortable with excess, particularly when it comes to praising others, preferring instead to understate. They also like a hint of criticism, believing that it is better to praise with faint damns. They also use wonderfully coded phrases that earn them the reputation for being perfidious. 'While Mr Smith was occasionally a little lapse in time keeping...' read 'he is habitually late'; 'Clearly growing out of earlier irresponsibility' means 'remains immature'; 'At her best with close friends ...' read 'socially unskilled with clients' and; 'got a well deserved lower second' should read is 'rather dull'. It is difficult to know whether this behaviour, namely writing in code, should be seen as pusillanimity in the face of having to give negative feedback or just a method of encoding messages for native speakers only. It means, of course, that when British employers write references that are sent overseas they should be aware of not being understood. Many also love the double-meaning found in phrases like: 'He left us fired with enthusiasm' or 'You will be very lucky to get her to work for you'.

Debrett's, that most celebrated of etiquette books, warns prospective hirers of good nannies: 'A too-brief letter of reference gives some clue to investigate further, and if a previous employer is less than enthusiastic about a former nanny a telephone chat will make the situation quite clear'. But will it? What reason is there to suppose that people who are tactful and diplomatic (ie, dishonest) in print can't or won't be the same on the telephone? A phone call may bring specific answers to specific questions but, unless the reference writer is scared of being sued, will give very much the same impression as the written reference. Indeed, if phone calls are more informative, why not use them instead of references right from the beginning?

The final problem lies in the motives of the reference writer. The loss of an employee has consequences — some good, some bad — and it is difficult to see how these might not influence the writer of a reference. Debrett's again on references for household staff states: 'When giving a reference, it is not fair to recommend an employee whom you would not employ yourself. On the other hand, it is essential to remember the importance of a good reference to someone seeking a household post, so even if you are smarting with annoyance you must be scrupulously fair and explain the good points of the applicant as well as the bad.' True enough, but rarely done. What a relief to hear that an incompetent and irascible employee is applying elsewhere. What a temptation it might be to put in a positive recommendation hoping that someone else will inherit your problems. This is a more common and more serious sin than writing a bad reference for a good employee who one may wish to retain. By definition, if they are good, employees will be clever enough to do well despite poor or even non-existent references.

Research studies in organizational behaviour and personnel psychology have shown that letters of reference on applicant competence are *not* predictive of future job performance. This is mainly due to the fact that they are too homogeneous with respect to the evaluation of applicant attributes and qualifications because everyone is characterised as 'somewhat desirable'. However, it has been observed that some negative comments among the positive may be seen as a sign of honesty on the part of the referee.

Many otherwise intelligent and sceptical employers and educationalists believe that with a modicum of common sense the process of selection is straightforward. The truth of the matter is far from it, as people who have studied the issue know even to their own cost. Outdated, invalid and corruptible methods are still used, and misplaced faith invested in them. Letters of reference are, in general, too susceptible to bias of one form or another to be of any real value in making the generally difficult decision of employee selection, appointment and promotion.

➤ References, testimonials and letters of recommendation are a standard part of the traditional job selection procedure.

➤ References take on a variety of forms; some are produced on pre-structured forms, while others are open-ended, optional texts.

➤ Lack of specificity in the way references are formatted can lead to data of questionable value in terms of judging a candidate's suitability for a job.

➤ References can contain hidden messages about candidates. The way things are said and what is omitted can be as informative as what is actually written.

B. Dressed for Success

Awareness of the potential for using clothing to enhance professional image has increased dramatically during the past ten years. The weak economy and tightening of many job markets has intensified interest in ways of creating the best impression in job interviews. With increased job competition in what, today, is an employer's market, it is becoming increasingly important for candidates to improve on the effectiveness of all aspects of their professional behaviour. Having the right qualifications may not be enough; it is essential to look the part as well. Knowing about the potential influence of dress can be vital for interviewees and interviewers alike.

Managers have been found openly to admit that appearance is important in forming important first impressions during job interviews, as well as when dealing with clients once on the job. One piece of American research reported that appearance ratings predicted nearly 70 per cent of judgements about job applicants. During the brief first impression situation, the interviewer must make use of any information available and attention is naturally drawn to the outward appearance of the person being interviewed. It is unfortunate perhaps that our first impressions, based upon how someone appears, can often colour our opinions about them subsequently in all kinds of situations. Hence, it is vitally important for job interviewees to get their appearance right on that very first meeting with a potential future employer.

When dress is part of the role demanded by a job, then evaluations based on appearance are obviously relevant. If an applicant is incompetent at dressing the part, the interviewer may have a legitimate reason to question the applicant's suitability for the job. In addition, appearance cues may become increasingly useful when information about applicants' experience and qualifications is minimal or incomplete. Research has indicated that the only times when style of dress is not taken into account in predicting likely future job performance is when evidence of impressive high previous achievement is available.

What kinds of dress therefore work best? One of the most important features is colour. Different values and connotations are attached to colours. This can therefore mean that by wearing certain colours these values and connotations can also attach themselves to a job applicant. Studies across more than one western industrialized country (e.g., Japan, United States) have revealed that darker colours are associated more significantly than lighter colours with perceptions of power and strength. To some extent darker colours are also seen as more lively and active, while lighter colours are seen as projecting a calmer, more reserved image.

American research among personnel staff responsible for recruiting new employees in over 150 organizations, ranging from small private businesses to large corporations, found that their judgements of female job applicants were significantly influenced by the colour of jacket they wore. Applicants, who were aged 19-21, were shown in photographs wearing either a dark jacket or a light jacket, and were either smiling or not smiling. Both facial expression and colour of jacket were important, but influenced the opinions of male and female personnel managers in different ways.

Male recruiters rated the women in dark jackets more favourably in terms of their perceived friendliness, while female recruiters thought that women wearing light jackets were the more sociable. These impressions were registered, however, only for applicants with a serious facial expression. Only male recruiters thought that applicants wearing dark jackets were more powerful and competent. The colour value of jackets made no difference to female recruiters' impressions of candidates on this dimension.

Another American study investigated the effects of style as well as colour of dress on impressions formed of male and female prospective job applicants. Applicants were assessed on four dimensions: self-assurance, likelihood of success in corporate life, properly attired for an executive, and likelihood of being chosen as an assistant. On this occasion, applicants were seen wearing either a blue or a red suit, and either with or without a jacket. Both the colour of dress and whether or not a jacket was being worn affected the perception of the applicant's competence.

Prospective job applicants who wore blue and had a jacket on were rated more highly. The colour factor, however, was not as significant for perceptions of women as for perceptions of men. While female applicants were rated somewhat lower on all dimensions when they wore red as opposed to blue, this difference was nothing like the one found for male applicants.

Male applicants wearing red were rated as significantly less self-assured, less likely to be successful, not so properly attired or less likely to be chosen compared to those dressed in blue. Interestingly, there was no apparent advantage for a woman wearing power red.

These findings support the idea that the standards of proper attire for men in the business world are increasingly being applied to women, but are still done so in a more relaxed manner. Clearly, wearing a jacket looks better for both sexes than turning up to an interview in shirt sleeves or a blouse. The effect of colour of dress, however, is more rigidly defined for men. Even so, in job markets where the supply of suitably qualified people exceeds demand, careful attention to style and colour of dress has emerged as an increasingly significant selection factor for both male and female job hunters. In a highly competitive selection situation, the way candidates dress for job interviews could very well make the difference between success and failure.

> In an increasingly competitive job market place, interviewees need to be aware of techniques designed to improve their performance.

> Job interviewers' early impressions of applicants in an interview can be significantly shaped by style of dress.

> A formal style of dress with jacket and the colour blue, as opposed to red, works best for male and to some extent for female candidates, in terms of favourable impression formation.

> Effects of colour of dress are more readily defined for men than for women.

> The influence of dress in the job selection context is important to know both for the interviewee and inteviewer.

C. Biodata:
Is there a Biography of Success?

We often call upon what we know about the way people have behaved in the past to forecast how they will perform in the future in all walks of life. In a business context many job interviews are dedicated almost exclusively to finding out how applicants behaved in their past employment. There is also a view that earlier experiences, perhaps at school or university, are equally revealing about a person's preferences, abilities, and competences.

For most of this century, recruiters have existed who stressed the importance of biographical factors (or 'biodata') in predicting occupational success. Astute factual questions can reveal a great deal. Our favourites include 'Are you a religious person?', and 'How far do you travel to work?' For all sorts of reasons, some recruiters reject the idea of using personality and ability tests, role-playing in assessment centres or rather vague, unfocused interviews. They favour instead a very well thought-out, relevant application form and perhaps a structured interview aimed at yielding answers to highly specific questions which are hoped to be predictive of occupational success.

There are some very clear advantages to the biodata approach. Biodata represent an alternative to the traditional selection or employment interview, with the advantage that every interviewee is asked the same question in exactly the same way, and the value judgements made by the interviewer are standardized, relevant, and of known validity.

There are distinct cost benefits as well. Although there may be fairly extensive research and development costs at the outset, once predictive questions have been identified, biodata are very cheap to use. Biodata forms can be developed in multiple-choice formats which are amenable to machine scoring or direct entry to a computer terminal. Thus, processing large numbers of applicants can become a routine clerical activity, freeing up the valuable time of personnel professionals or line managers.

The standards set in using biodata are objective and consistent. Reading through application forms is an extremely tedious activity. It is often shared by a number of managers, who may not set precisely the same standards or use the same criteria. This is especially true where similar jobs are being filled across a number of locations or offices, or when recruitment takes place only at specific times of year. The biodata approach allows for basic standards to be set objectively and with total consistency.

23

Minorities can be identified and treated fairly. In setting up a biodata form, the link between the information on the form and suitability for the job needs to be established. This, in itself, tends to ensure that irrelevant factors are excluded from the selection process. In addition, the research necessary to construct the application form can provide the basis for setting up and monitoring an equal opportunities programme. Biodata forms, especially when computer scored, are completely blind to incidental items such as personal names which might indicate ethnic background.

finally, although biodata application forms have not always delivered the same level of predictive accuracy in practical usage as have been obtained in academic experimentation, their track record is still good. Compared to the unstructured interview, which is a typical alternative, or to reading an application form in an unstructured way, they can produce increases in selection success rates of many orders of magnitude.

Any method used to select, promote, or remove employees naturally attracts a great deal of examination and criticism. The use of biodata is no exception. Some of the more important objections include:

● **Too much of the same.** If many biographical items are used in selection, the organization inevitably becomes more homogeneous over time, which has both advantages and disadvantages. Heterogeneity may occur across organizational divisions with different criteria but not within them. A biographically-homogeneous organization may be a time bomb if for some reason the criteria upon which all employees are chosen no longer predict success; indeed such a procedure may have the opposite effect. That is, it is all right selecting very similar individuals who are virtually identical on the factors which predict success. But what if the criteria change and one has a whole organization of people with irrelevant, even dysfunctional skills?

● **Cloning the past.** Biodata work on the idea that past behaviour predicts current performance, but if current criteria are very unstable (say in a rapidly changing market), a biodata instrument may quickly get out of date. Biodata may be best in stable organizations and environments, of which there are increasingly fewer.

● **Faking.** Biodata measures have been shown to be fakeable. One researcher checked information given by applicants for a nursing aide post with previous employers. Half the sample overestimated how long they had worked for their previous employer. Overstating previous salary, and describing part-time work as full-time were also common. More seriously, one in four applicants gave reasons for leaving with which their previous employer did not agree, and no less than seventeen per cent gave as their last employer someone who had never heard of them. In principle, all biodata answers can be checked (by positive vetting) but employees know that this can take a long time and that many potential employees won't bother to run thorough checks. Hence they can and do risk faking.

● **Fairness in the law.** If sex, age and race are shown to be major biographical determinates, it is tempting to select in and select out particular groups. This would, of course, be illegal. Items such as age, sex and marital status may in fact be challenged in the courts, if such items are included in inventories for the purpose of personnel selection. In that event, whatever gains in predictive power are derived through the inclusion of these items must be weighed against legal considerations.

● **Biodata don't travel well.** The same criteria do not invariably have the same predictability across jobs, organizations, or time periods. Because new criteria have to be established for each situation, the development of biodata can be expensive and tedious. Just as the criteria of success change, so do the factors that predict them.

● **Atheoretical.** The major disadvantage of biodata, being entirely empirical and non-theoretical, is that it is difficult to know which of a myriad of biographical factors to choose. Theory-based approaches can explain which factors predict job success and help choose which ones to use in different situations. Biodata rejoice in being unencumbered by theory: they represent a 'suck it and see' approach which looks quite simply at biographical correlates of measurable job success.

● **Time-consuming.** Most biographical selection criteria are chosen using data from applicants. The disadvantage of this is that it is very time-consuming. It might, for example, take at least twelve months to obtain reliable, meaningful performance results on new employees. If an organization does not have a regular intake of new staff, there could be a two- or three-year delay between sending the draft biodata form to applicants and obtaining a large enough sample of employees to warrant further development work. This problem of establishing the predictive validity of a biodata instrument can be circumvented by identifying which biodata criteria are the best discriminators between current employees who are high performers and low performers.

● **Shrinkage over time.** Biodata scoring keys do not appear to hold up indefinitely. There is evidence that the validity of biodata shrinks over time, and periodic re-validation and re-weighting may be necessary. This can be costly and time-consuming. Also, one cannot predict which items hold up over time or why. In general, the evidence suggests that the shelf-life of biodata is between three and five years. It is probably good practice to re-test any selection process every couple of years but biodata necessitates it.

But biodata remain an alternative, cost-effective means of selection. For instance, one airline found two factors which very clearly distinguished between above and below average cabin crew. These were how much the attendants had lived or travelled abroad before the age of twelve and whether their parents had separated or divorced. In another study, some of the best predictors of success in the financial sector were the presence of a home computer, the age of marriage, the size of mortgage and sociable extra-curricular activities. If an employer knows that certain biographical details (A—levels obtained; age at first marriage; size of mortgage) are predictors of occupational success in a particular job, gathering and weighting the data must add significantly to the accuracy of selection. Many of the above problems can be dealt with successfully and the method represents a sensible, cost-effective, and tested means of selecting employees.

➤ Biodata (or biographical data), that is verifiable, actual occurrences in a person's life, are among the best predictors of business success.

➤ This method involves correlating a range of biographical experiences with important, measurable business success criteria, retaining and weighting those that do distinguish significantly between good and poor performers and devising an application form based exclusively on them.

➤ Like all other selection methods, biodata do have certain limitations but these can largely be overcome.

➤ The use of biodata is particularly appealing as a method to those who distrust business or psychological theories and 'soft' personality tests.

D. Business and Pleasure: What Free Time Activities Don't Tell Us About People

'What are your leisure pursuits and hobbies?' This is a very common interview question and one that has nearly always been asked already in the application form. It provides a wonderful opportunity, of course, for self-aggrandizement and impression management. ('Crosswords, computers and lacrosse' is meant to indicate 'I am literate, numerate and sporty', while 'Numismatics and ichthyology' means 'I am pretentious, collect coins and have a fish tank.' 'Train-spotting and fishing' probably means 'I am honest'.)

filling out this section in the application form is usually pleasurable, but may pose problems. Some people do not have leisure activities in a conventional sense; 'pontificating at dinner parties' or 'pottering round the house' don't usually qualify. For others, work is their major passion: Sir Peter Hall, the theatre director, for example, on being asked what his leisure time activities were, replied 'Leisure? What need I of other pastimes when I enjoy my work so!' The other concern is being caught out. It is all very well putting down 'modern jazz dancing' or 'cuckoo-clock carving' to impress, but what if there is an expert across that table who knows more about the subject than you?

In fact, studies of what people *actually* do reveal us to be a pretty dull lot. Data reported in Social Trends (the British survey results) 1985, relating to the daily activities of the 'average Briton', indicated that our most popular pastimes include listening to records/tapes, reading books, and going out for a drink. Furthermore we spend about twenty four hours a week (just under four hours a day) watching the box. Walking is the most popular 'sport', followed by snooker/billiards, then darts. And yet we are supposed to 'self-actualise', reach our full potential, though leisure. According to Samuel Johnson, 'All intellectual improvement arises in leisure', while Disraeli opined that 'Increased means and increased leisure are the two civilisers of man'. Even the Bible (Ecclesiasticus, 38:4) asserts that 'The wisdom of a learned man cometh by opportunity of leisure: and he that hath little business shall become wise' (that, of course, was before the boozer and the box were invented.)

Most people seem to think that an individual's choice of leisure pursuits provides a unique and very insightful perspective on personality; a sort of royal road to the real person. That is, they reveal a person's needs, motives, or habits. Thus extraverts, it is suggested, choose highly arousing, sociable, varied activities (disco dancing, amateur dramatics), while introverts prefer passive, retiring, familiar activities (reading, collecting, computing).

However, this belief overlooks two important points. first, as left-wingers are wont to point out, we rarely have true choice. Often age, sex, income and place of abode preclude various leisure activities. It is very costly to go ballooning or parachuting; rugby may be dangerous after forty; it is difficult to be a committed hill walker if one lives in Central London. Thus, even though we might want to participate in a particular leisure activity (which might or might not reflect one's personality), we may be prevented from doing so by circumstances beyond our control.

Secondly, a person's choice of occupation may also reflect needs. Thus, subject to the constraints outlined above, those who have high nurturance needs may choose the medical profession; those with needs for order and silence, librarianship; the need for avarice may be fulfilled in the City; the need for power in Parliament. To the extent that a person's needs are fulfilled at work, he/she may be less driven to pursue his or her fulfilment elsewhere, in which case leisure activities might be expected to reflect personality striving only marginally, if at all.

This notion is implicit in one or two, mutually contradictory, theories of work and leisure currently in vogue. According to 'Compensation Theory', leisure and work experiences are *antithetical* with such jargon terms as 'complementarity', 'competition', 'regeneration', or even 'heteromorphism' are used by academics to convey the idea that people choose leisure time activities to compensate and fulfil needs that are frustrated by work. So-called 'Spillover Theory', on the other hand, emphasizes the fundamental *similarity* between work and leisure. Jargon terms in this instance include 'generalisation', 'familiarity', 'isomorphism', 'continuation' and 'congruence'. The idea is that one chooses one's work to fulfil needs (drives, ambitions etc.), but this being only partially successful, one spends one's leisure time 'topping up'.

In other words, if the compensation theory is true, the last thing the motor car worker wishes to do is to spend the weekend doing mechanical work, whereas if the spillover theory is true, he can't wait to repair his own or his neighbour's car (or, indeed, assemble a car that he has carefully brought through the gates part-by-part in his lunch box).

Do people in fact 'spill over' or 'compensate' (or neither or both)? Any copy of Who's Who provides a semi-random sample of its distinguished decision makers. Most entrants specify their leisure time pursuits. They differ enormously. Some people use this as a vehicle for further self-aggrandizement (Donald Sinden, the actor, lists French History and Ecclesiology, and Cyril Smith, the politician, Charitable Works), while others show they have a sense of humour (John Cleese, the comic, lists Gluttony and Sloth, Frank Muir, the writer, 'Staring silently into space', and Frederic Raphael, the writer, 'Painting things white'). The vast majority, however, are curt and factual. An analysis of entries showed music to be very popular, but gardening came out top.

Why gardening? In fact gardening provides the answer for Compensation Theory. It is important to point out that Who's Who entrants have a lot in common, not least that they are all 'Decision-Makers'. They sit on boards, committees, think-tanks, or councils all day long, discussing, debating, domineering and doodling. And therein lies the compensatory attraction of pottering around in one's garden.

Gardening for these Who's Whoers is a private, solo activity. Not for them the bonhomie and camaraderie of the allotment where working-class men escape their wives and families and enjoy the odd glass of home-made beer carefully stored next to the manure in the potting shed. Gardening for these Decision-Makers is a private, quiet activity away from other people and the drone of the board-room.

Secondly, it is physically demanding exercise that, quite literally, gets one's hands dirty. This is a nice compensation for those whose major exercise is pushing paper from left to right across smooth, well-polished oak and leather-topped desks or opening a nice claret. Being physically tired from hard labour is a refreshing change from the exhaustion of a day on a committee or in a plane where the very constraint on movement is itself exhausting. Getting dirty or being messy even is more delightfully antithetical to a daily work routine which can be construed as a never-ending battle to impose order on potential chaos, ie, to combat messiness, a legitimate outlet for which Freud would have termed 'anal' impulses.

Thirdly, and perhaps most importantly, gardening offers one the opportunity of activity producing something, and relatively quickly. Decision-Makers are frequently responsible for galvanising others into action and instigating programmes that ultimately achieve or produce something. But the time-spans are often excessively long, a bit like being an architect for a never-finished cathedral or Pyramid. Sometimes, indeed often, one never sees the product of one's labours. The Marxist's alienation argument may apply here. Like the car worker on the conveyer belt who only screws in the rear parking light, and never identifies with the completed vehicle that emerges shining and finished at the other end, the Decision-Maker may never identify with the final product that emerges (e.g., degree course, new factory in South East Asia).

And therein lies the advantage of tomato growing. One can buy the seeds, water, weed and fertilize them and, within a relatively short period of time (usually just when those red and round Dutch and Jersey tomatoes are cheapest in the shops), harvest those small, speckled, gnarled objects which may be proudly displayed as the centre-piece of the Sunday luncheon party.

There is one other possibility. Some people garden by planting oaks, by landscaping, by actually changing the environment. Michael Heseltine, the politician, is one such latter-day Capability Brown. For them, gardening is one way of making a lasting contribution to the future; a living monument. One's life among the stocks and shares or on committees may provide money, but in many senses it is utterly ephemeral, merely the creation and circulation of paper. But to plant and tender great trees that will continue to grow and blossom long after one is dead, *that* has real worth.

But what of the evidence for spillover? The librarian who comes home looking forward to a quiet evening with a book; the car-worker who downs tools on his car plant to take up an identical (borrowed?) set to tinker about with his car; the cook who leaves the over-priced health food restaurant to spend an enthralled evening at a vegetarian cookery class?

The problem is that, ultimately, one really has no way of knowing which theory is true in any given case. It is a little like resolving the issue of the truthfulness of antonymous proverbs: 'Out of sight, out of mind'; 'Absence makes the heart grow fonder'. It is quite possible that *both* are true, but in different circumstances.

The royal road to understanding other people's personalities is clearly *not* via an exposé of their leisure time activities. The main function of leisure questions on application forms is probably to provide interviewers both with something to talk about when they are at a loss, and with an opportunity for legitimate voyeurism.

➤ During the selection process candidates are often asked to supply details about hobbies and leisure pursuits. This information tends to be understood or utilised ineffectively.

➤ Only careful and informed analysis of leisure activities can provide valuable insights into the type of person a candidate is and hence their suitability for a job.

E. Personality Testing

After twenty years of ostracism and cynicism, personality and ability testing has become popular, even mandatory, in many organizations.

Regular surveys of British, European and American companies indicate that between a quarter and a third use psychological tests and that the number is generally increasing. However, academic psychologists remain highly sceptical about the predictive validity of any, or all, personality tests, particularly in the market-place of work.

A little of this scepticism, even cynicism, has rubbed off on personnel and human resources directors, but many remain eager to buy and apply such tests to selection and related organizational issues.

It is not difficult to see why business people are attracted to the idea of testing. Establishing an accurate, fair and sensitive process of selection and appraisal is far from easy. Everyone has experienced the awkward, or inadequate, or lazy, or irresponsible, or inefficient colleague whom somebody selected and nobody can sack. As a result some use tests specifically to select out, rather than select in: to warn about people who may prove problematic, rather than highlight potential high-flyers.

It is difficult to obtain all relevant information about people, compare them with others and make judgments on their future success only by referring to CVs and interviewing them, so it is no surprise that managers turn to personality tests which are apparently scientific, seem to provide useful material on a whole range of personality traits and give normative data for the population as a whole.

On the other hand, there are those who believe that with sufficient experience and a modicum of common sense they can easily select the right person. Tests are not for them. They might argue that just as intelligence tests do not measure intelligence, so personality tests can hardly measure something as complex, subtle and varied as personality. After all, people have one thing in common — they are all different; so some feel it offensive to reduce people to sets of sixteen numbers on a computer-generated profile.

In fact as more and more personality tests come on to the market, cynics have had to rehearse their arguments more frequently. Common objections are:

● Many of these tests can be faked. People may lie to put themselves in a good light and achieve high scores, but this does not reflect their real personality.

31

● Some people do not have sufficient self-insight to report on their own feelings and behaviour. Some cannot, rather than will not, give accurate answers about themselves.

● Tests are unreliable in that all sorts of temporary factors such as anxiety, boredom, weariness or ill-health can lead people to give different answers on different occasions. Tests give inconsistent or unstable character profiles.

● Tests lack validity as they do not measure what they purport to measure and, equally, the scores do not predict performance in business over time. Many tests have this Achilles heel and are lamentably short of robust proof of their validity.

● Tests might be able to measure all sorts of dimensions of behaviour but not those crucial to the organization such as trustworthiness and likelihood of absenteeism. Buying personality tests is like having a set menu; what many managers want is the *à la carte*, where they can select what they want.

● People have to be sufficiently literature or articulate to do the tests and be sufficiently familiar with North American jargon. Many organizations believe their work-force could not do them properly, it would take up too much time or would cause embarrassment.

● There are no good norms, at least for the populations companies want to test; comparing them with North American samples, mostly white undergraduates, is dangerously misleading. That is, there are no benchmark statistics against which to measure employees.

● The tests are unfair and biased in favour of the white middle class, thus white males tend to do better or show more attractive profiles and so get selected. Many tests are the product of middle-class, middle-brow, middle-aged, middle Americans and are not appropriate for those from other groups.

● Interpretation of the tests takes skill, insight and experience which may be too expensive or not available. In the wrong hands, tests are dangerous because profiles are given inaccurate or too literal interpretations. Organizations can become consultant dependent, which is a very expensive addiction.

● Freedom of information legislation may mean that candidates can see and perhaps challenge the scores themselves, the way scores are interpreted or the decisions made on them. This may lead to extreme embarrassment or, worse, litigation.

● As tests of both ability and personality become well known, people could buy copies and practise so that they know the correct or most desirable answers. This happens extensively with US ability testing and results could be seen to have more to do with preparation and practice than actual ability.

These eleven criticisms are frequently heard. In some instances, and considering some tests, they are more than justified. They make a useful list with which to confront a testing enthusiast. But old hands know most of the answers and can provide impressive statistics on norms, reliability and so on. In addition to answering the criticisms they may also in fact present a strong case for testing. Examples are:

● Tests provide numeric information which means individuals can more easily be compared on the same criteria. Different questions are asked of different candidates during interviews and the answers often forgotten. Testing is an empirical, scientific operation.

● With data-based records a person's development can be traced over time. Test results in an individual's file can actually demonstrate if, and by how much, the tests were predictive of later work-related behaviour.

● Tests give explicit and specific results on temperament and ability rather than the vague, ambiguous, coded platitudes so often found in references. A percentage score, provided of course that it is valid, makes for much clearer thinking about personal characteristics than terms such as satisfactory, sufficient, or high-flyer.

● Tests are fair because they eliminate corruption and stop favouritism or old boy, masonic or Oxbridge networks from self perpetuating. That is, if a person does not have the ability or has a 'dangerous' profile, they will not be chosen irrespective of their other 'assets'.

● Tests are comprehensive in that they cover all the basic dimensions of personality and ability from which other behaviour patterns derive. Most, but not all, tests tap into the agreed three crucial facets of human personality which are extraversion, stability and tough-mindedness.

● Tests are scientific in that they are soundly empirically based on proven theoretical foundations. That is, they are reliable, valid and able to discriminate the good from the mediocre and the average from the bad. Many have a wealth of studies in their support 'proving' that personality/ability scores relate to occupational behaviour.

➤ Personality testing is not a panacea to all selectors' needs. Not only are there many non-validated tests on the market, but also many personnel professionals don't know how to use them.

➤ Chosen wisely, by content and not packaging, certain personality tests, however, can help to detect and pin-point important psychological facets of employees.

➤ Nevertheless, all tests have potentially very important limitations which must be recognized.

➤ Used judiciously as part of a package of assessment methods tests can add unique and insightful data in the process of selection.

F. The Writing in the Stars: Why so Many (Otherwise Intelligent) People Believe in the Validity of Astrology and Graphology

Why, despite their irreconcilability with either scientific rationalism and Christian beliefs, as well as a highly dubious reliability record, do so many people from all backgrounds believe in, consult and act upon astrological and graphological predictions? Some businesses in Britain use the services of a graphologist while the French frequently consult astrologers. Social scientists have considered seriously the possibility that there is some validity in these predictions, yet patient, presuppositionless research on the part of disinterested researchers has by and large failed to find any replicable theoretically-based or explicable significant findings. This is perhaps far more true of graphology than of astrology for which there is equivocal evidence. Both are falsifiable and both have been falsified, yet people still believe. In short graphology and astrology are bunk. Yet so many people are hoodwinked. Why?

There are two sorts of answers to this question. One concerns the reliability and validity of alternative, more acceptable, ways of assessing, describing or measuring people. High unemployment has meant unprecedented numbers of people applying for jobs and bewildered selectors are turning to any means of assessment they can trust. Some believe in school grades or the predictiveness of leisure pursuits (always the source of greatest lies in an application form) despite the evidence that they are weak predictors of occupational success. Indeed there is some evidence to suggest that there may be a reverse correlation between success in some A-level subjects and occupational competence and promotion. Others have consulted occupational psychologists, whose carefully constructed psychometric tests certainly have the appearance of objective scientific measures. However, British distrust of psychology, the emergence of numerous fairly bogus consultancies, and the excessive use of poorly psychometrised tests means that both because of the costs and the poor performance of some of these tests, distraught and over-burdened selectors are turning elsewhere. Many have turned to graphology. Newspaper reports frequently quote a number of important, influential and possibly intelligent people who believe in, and hence use, graphology in selection. This is the case despite literally dozens of scientific studies that again and again challenge the validity of graphology accurately to describe personality or predict behaviour.

However, the more plausible reason why people believe in graphology and astrology is paradoxical. The reason why people believe in graphological and astrological interpretations or readings is because they *are* true, but and it is an important but, they are vague positive generalisations with high base rate validity (ie, true of most people) yet are supposedly derived specifically for a named person.

For nearly forty years psychologists have been investigating the Barnum Effect. It was the famous circus-act producer Phineas T. Barnum who said 'There's a sucker born every minute', and had as his formula of success 'A little something for everybody'. The Barnum Effect refers to the phenomenon whereby people accept personality feedback about themselves, whether it is universally valid or trivial, because it is supposedly derived from personality assessment procedures. In other words people believe in astrology and graphology because they fall victim to the fallacy of personal validation, which means that people accept the generalisation of trite bogus descriptions which are true of nearly everybody, to be specifically true of themselves.

Consider a psychological study to illustrate this point. An American psychologist called Stagner gave a group of personnel managers a well-established personality test. But instead of scoring it and giving them the actual results, he gave each of them bogus feedback in the form of thirteen statements derived from horoscopes, graphological analyses and so on. Each manager was then asked to read over the feedback (supposedly derived for him/herself from the 'scientific' test) and decide how accurate the assessment was by marking each sentence on a scale of (a) Amazingly accurate; (b) Rather good; (c) About half and half; (d) More Wrong than Right; (e) Almost entirely wrong. The table shows the results . Over half felt their profile was an amazingly accurate description of them, while forty per cent thought it was rather good. Almost none believed it to be very wrong.

A glance at the items reveals exactly the process. If you add together the first two columns and look at those two considered most accurate 'You prefer a certain amount of change and variety and become dissatisfied when hemmed in by restrictions and limitations' and 'While you have personality weaknesses you are generally able to compensate for them', and least accurate 'Your sexual adjustment has presented problems for you' and 'some of your aspirations tend to be pretty unrealistic' you see the importance of positive general feedback. People definitely and not unnaturally have a penchant for the positive.

Many researchers have replicated this result. A French psychologist advertised his services as an astrologer in various newspapers and got back hundreds of requests for his service. He replied to each letter by sending out mimeographed identical copies of single, ambiguous, 'horoscopes'. More than two hundred clearly gullible clients actually wrote back praising his accuracy and perceptiveness. A psychology lecturer in New Zealand regularly gets his naïve first year students to write down in frank detail their dreams, or he might ask them to describe in detail what they see in an inkblot, the more mystical the task the better. A week later he gives them the thirteen statements shown in the table and gets them to rate these items. Only after they have publicly declared their belief in the test are they encouraged to swop feedback. The humiliation of being so easily fooled is a powerful learning experience.

Research on the Barnum Effect has, however, shown that beliefs in this bogus feedback situation are influenced by a number of important factors, some to do with the client and the consultant (their personality, naïvety, etc), and some to do with the nature of the test and the feedback situation itself. Curiously, client (naïve purchaser) and consultant (astrologer, graphologist) factors have shown comparatively few results. Women are not more susceptible than men, though of course generally naïve or gullible people are (tautologically!) more susceptible to this effect. Furthermore, the status and prestige of the consultant are only marginally important, which is of course good news for the more bogus people in this field.

However, some variables are crucial. One of the most important is *perceived specificity* of the information required. The more detailed the question the better, so you have to specify exact time, date and place of birth to astrologers. In one study, an American researcher gave all his subjects the same horoscope and found that those who were told that the interpretation was based on the year, month and day of birth judged it to be more accurate than those who were led to believe that it was based only on the year and month. Again and again studies show that after people receive general statements they think pertain *just* to them, their faith in the procedure and in the diagnostician increases. A client's satisfaction is no measure of how well the diagnostician has differentiated him or her from others, but it is utterly dependent on the extent to which they believe the feedback is specific to them.

The second factor belies the truth that we are all hungry for compliments but sceptical of criticism; that is the feedback must be favourable. It need not to be entirely, utterly positive but if it is by and large positive with the occasional mildly negative comment (that itself may be a compliment), people will believe it. This can easily be demonstrated by giving the well-used thirteen statements in the table with the opposite primarily negative meaning (ie. 'You do not pride yourself as an independent thinker and accept others' statements without satisfactory proof'). This confirms another prin-

Evaluations of Items by 68 Personnel Managers When Presented as a 'Personality' Analysis

	Judgment as to Accuracy of Item-Percent[1] Choosing				
	a[2]	b	c	d	e
A You have a great need for other people to like and admire you.	39	46	13	1	1
B You have a tendency to be critical of yourself.	46	36	15	3	0
C You have a great deal of unused capacity which you have not turned to your advantage.	37	36	18	1	4
D While you have some personality weaknesses, you are generally able to compensate for them.	34	55	9	0	0
E Your sexual adjustment has presented problems for you.	15	16	16	33	19
F Disciplined and self-controlled outside, you tend to be worrisome and insecure inside.	40	21	22	10	4
G At times you have serious doubts as to whether you have made the right decision or done the right thing.	37	31	19	18	4
H You prefer a certain amount of change and variety and become dissatisfied when hemmed in by restrictions and limitations.	63	28	7	1	1
I You pride yourself as an independent thinker and do not accept others' statements without satisfactory proof.	49	32	12	4	4
J You have found it unwise to be frank in revealing yourself to others.	31	37	22	6	4
K At times you are extraverted, affable, sociable, while at other times you are introverted, wary, reserved.	43	25	18	9	5
L Some of your aspirations tend to be pretty unrealistic.	12	16	22	43	7
M Security is one of your major goals in life.	40	31	15	9	5

1. Not all percentages add up to 100% because of omissions by an occasional subject.

2. Definitions of scale steps as follows:
   a. amazingly accurate
   b. rather good
   c. about half and half
   d. more wrong than right
   e. almost entirely wrong

ciple in personality measurement: the Pollyanna Principle which suggests that there is a universal human tendency to use or accept positive words or feedback more frequently, diversely and facilely than negative words and feedback. It has been shown that according to the evaluation of two judges there were five times as many favourable as unfavourable statements in highly acceptable interpretations and twice as many unfavourable statements in rarely acceptable interpretations.

It is not difficult to explain the popularity of astrology and graphology. The lengthy feedback is based on specific information (time and place of birth for astrology; slant and size of writing, correctness of letters, dotting of i's and crossing of t's, use of loops, etc, in graphology). It is nearly always favourable. Take, for example, the analysis of a prominent British politician's writing published in a quality newspaper. 'Optimistic, Forward-looking, Extrovert, Intelligent. Appreciative of the Arts, Cultured, Decisive, Signs of stubbornness, Quick mind, but not good with trivia; needs people to whom he can delegate.' A typical example of general positive statements applicable to between five and ten million people in this country. And note the praising with faint damns 'Signs of Stubbornness' (not signs of intelligence, but of stubbornness) and 'not good with trivia'. Also it is often the troubled (worried, depressed, insecure) who visit astrologers, graphologists or fortune tellers. They are particularly sensitive to objective, positive information about themselves and the future. Therefore, the very type of feedback and the predisposition of clients make the acceptance highly probable. This also accounts for the popularity of astrological books; your stars foretell columns in books; the I Ching etc. Each offers fairly long descriptions of each sun-sign type in positive, general terms but with the caveat and a warning that the description is only an approximation and that an accurate description can only be obtained from a specific cast horoscope. But if the general description seems true (and it probably is), people frequently conclude that it must be even more true when even more specific information is used. Furthermore, this process is enhanced over time for two reasons. Since Freud it has been known that people selectively remember more positive events about themselves than negative and are thus likely to remember more feedback that coincides with their own views of themselves than information that is less relevant or contradictory to it. Secondly, of course, people have to pay for the consultation. Perhaps one needs a wealth warning in every astrological statement.

There are other attractions of astrological and graphological reading. They not only give useful, fascinating information about oneself, but they, also predict the future so reducing anxieties and uncertainties about what will happen. Also, unlike other forms of therapy which require psychological work and/or behaviour change to obtain any benefit, in graphology one merely has to supply a writing specimen, or in astrology the exact time and place of birth. There is much to gain and little to lose at the astrologist/graphologist. Not surprisingly then a comfortable collaborative illusion of scientific validity emerges, formed between the buyer and seller of the astrological reading and handwriting analyses.

finally, there is one other reason why people value graphology and astrology — the self-fulfilling prophecy. It is quite possible that if one is told 'As a Virgo, you are particularly honest'; this may lead one to notice and subsequently selectively recall all or any, albeit trivial, instances of behavioural confirmation (pointing out that a person had dropped a bus ticket; giving back excess change). The self-fulfilling prophecy may work on both a conceptual and a behavioural basis. Thus Virgos come to include the trait of honesty in their self-concept but also they may actually become slightly or occasionally more honest. Thus, graphology and astrology predictions may come true because they partly dictate them!

Beware the fortune cookie, the graphologist and the astrologer! The moral of the story, of course, is that you can impress anyone with the perspicacity of your psychological insights as long as they are vague, relevant for most people, generally favourable, but personalised just for you. Fortune tellers have exploited this fact for hundreds of years. Crystal balls have been replaced by tarot cards or simple pen and ink, but the principle remains the same: 'The fault of false belief, dear Reader, is not in our stars, it is in ourselves'.

➤ Many business people faced with the acknowledged difficult job of selection turn to the possibility of astrology, graphology, and other bogus 'ologies'.

➤ It is easy to see why they become duped believers because doing the test themselves they tend to receive bland positive feedback that makes them feel good about themselves.

➤ People do not realize that much of this feedback is true ... but is true of everybody.

➤ Ask graphologistss to predict sex, age, occupation, etc., of any person and they decline, knowing how easy it will be to catch them on these criteria. They prefer the murky, vague and easily fudgeable world of personality.

2
TRAINING AND DEVELOPMENT

Nearly all organizations invest in the training and development of their staff. They believe, presumably, that all staff members need training in new techniques and approaches, and that the best can only be got out of them if they are sent regularly on various courses.

This section takes a measured and, occasionally sceptical, look at the whole business of management training. It also looks at current trends in this area. Among the trends we have chosen to examine are outdoor training, assessment centres, the use of mentors and the use of television and videos.

Training is not the same as teaching and the two are contrasted. Training can be as much about socialization into the company culture and values as it is about the acquisition of new skills. This issue is also touched on.

Training and development can and often does eatup a large proportion of an organization's human resource budget. It is therefore most important that it is chosen and executed wisely.

A. Attitudes to Management Training

Management training courses are big business. In 1991 American companies spent over $1 billion in sending their employees on courses. The sheer amount of unsolicited mail advertising courses in Britain attests to their increasing popularity.

Management training courses differ enormously: some are conducted in-house, others run outside the organization; some are very long (three weeks or more), others are simply a day long (or even less); some take place in plush hotels, others in the open air; some are instruction-based, others are experiential; some participants are volunteers, others conscripts. Despite their variety they all have one thing in common: they cost money, lots of money, particularly if you take into consideration the opportunity costs involved by calculating the amount lost through the participants not working.

Management training is now a huge industry. Consultancy companies, magazines, and human resource departments are exclusively dedicated to teaching people how to manage; and how to manage more effectively and efficiently. The newly inducted, the freshly promoted, the diagnosed incompetent as well as the high-flyer are sent on these ubiquitous and manifold courses on such topics as time management, communication skills, finance for non-specialists, negotiation skills and much more.

But do these courses work? That is, can they be measured in some way and be shown to have a desirable effect? In short, what is the point of management training?

A lot of blood, sweat, tears and ink has been spilled over this apparently simple question. Hard-headed types, those who point out bottom-line criteria, want evidence that the expense is justified by increased productivity and hence revenue. On the other hand, cuddly, warm, human resource managers seem happy enough if they get the feeling, through ratings on a feedback form that participants have enjoyed the course.

A variety of arguments and statistics are paraded on both sides regarding the efficiency of management training. However, it is possible to identify four quite different and distinct camps or positions taken by members of various persuasions.

Cynics will have nothing to do with management training if they can help it. They tend to believe that it is a waste of time and a completely pointless exercise. They resent what they regard as smug, smart, management consultants nosing into their organizations and despise seeing course-junkies on yet another jolly junket away from the office. They hold the view that either management practices are learnt through experience, that rather nebulous concept meaning doing the same thing for a very long time or (simultaneously and paradoxically) that they cannot be taught. Many believe that people are basically untrainable anyway. Therefore they certainly do not take seriously all the evidence that training works arguing that what can be taught is not important and equally what is teachable is not relevant. Cynics see management trainers as vacuous gurus, posers and overpaid, underworked people who are either without managerial experience themselves or failed managers. Those who can, manage, and those who can't become management trainers.

Sceptics are less hostile to management training but far from eager for it for themselves or their staff. Many believe they (their supervisors and subordinates) could manage better. They recognise that training courses might help. But they also know that these courses are highly variable in content, style and effect and that many are flavour of the month, hot-air jargon that is really neither clear nor helpful. Thus, they tend to stay away from the soft interpersonal sorts of courses, preferring the more serious financial skills, computer literacy sorts of courses. Some reluctantly believe that you have to send people on courses because they expect it, but they would really prefer not to. They argue with some conviction that even if courses are beneficial, the benefits soon wear off. Unpractised skill deteriorates. Back in the work place the idealistic practices are ignored or even punished and hence not continued. Most believe the solution lies in selecting people who are already well-trained or at least trainable. Many sceptics argue that you change and develop an organization through its structure or reward system. You cannot do it through the quick-fix of sending selected individuals on courses.

Enthusiasts will have nothing of this. They simply cannot see how people are expected to manage without being explicitly taught and trained. Most are benevolently eclectic in the types of methods they advocate, though others are zealous about a specific type of course or approach. They both reward course attendance and use it as a reward. Optimists argue that training is a major source of changing, improving and updating a company. Many argue that there is no alternative: managing is a skill and must be learnt. It is cost-effective to train people because although they do learn by experience, this is just a shorthand for slow, lazy, inefficient and expensive learning. Training enthusiasts advocate a judicious review and audit of the training needs of particular organizations, an appraisal and 'which' guide analysis of all the courses available, followed by a time-tabling of people on courses. Enthusiasts are not against a rigorous post-course analysis to determine quality, suitability and so on. But they are believers in potential value of courses and, in some instances, their absolute necessity.

Naïve proponents have an evangelical air about the way they push courses.

They are proselytizers of the near-miraculous benefits of such-and-such a course, test, guru or concept. If only, they argue, people were to go on a course, understand and live its message, all would be well with the organization. Naïve proponents certainly don't seek hard evidence for the benefits of training courses. Personal testimony and evidence will do for that. Fortunately, selective hearing and memory means they carry around in their heads only the successful stories of the Lourdes-like change of an individual before and after attending a course. They have the Dickensian idea of managers being vessels that need to be topped up with the rich and invigorating liquor of training courses. They assume a direct relationship between brochure quality and glossiness and course quality, and many innocently assume that all aims and goals will be met by the course tutor. Naïve proponents admire and often envy course leaders, tutors, facilitators or whatever they are called. Many even try their hand at it. It is not easy to stop the converted preaching. Naïve proponents are found in all organizations, big and small scale, services and manufacturing, and their numbers are growing.

To the management training courses cynic, the naïve proponent is a pathetic money-wasting air head, while the latter sees the former as a sour boor. Inevitably, there are more enthusiasts in personnel and human resources and more sceptics in accounts and engineering departments, but there are exceptions to this rule.

To some degree people who hold these different attitudes are interested in, and attracted to, different types of management courses which have quite diverse aims and hoped-for outcomes. To this extent the different types are thinking about different types of courses rather than management training in general.

There are essentially two types of people in the world; those who believe in two types and those who don't. Of course typologies can be fun but misleadingly simple. Very often people's reactions to training are a mix. In the end, one can only hope there are more sceptical enthusiasts than naïve cynics about.

➤ The variety of business related training courses run by individuals, colleges and consultancies is on the increase. Some organizations believe it is important and cost-effective enough to have an in-house training department.

➤ Specific, highly relevant job-related skills, general management skills and somewhat vaguer communication or personal improvement courses are available.

➤ Reactions to training courses are not uniform, though various trends can be detected. At the one extreme are cynics who believe them to be nearly all useless and a waste of money. Diametrically opposed to them are naïve optimists who believe they can have near-miraculous effects on select individuals and the organization as a whole.

➤ Clearly it is unwise to make generalizations about courses. People have to be trained as well as learning through the on-the-job apprenticeship method. Training courses need to be carefully selected, audited and tested for effectiveness.

➤ Most importantly there needs to be a good fit between the content, aims, style and pace of the training course and the needs of the individual and the organization as a whole.

B. Trends in Training

Big organizations still have comparatively large training budgets. They buy in, or have in-house training departments, centres, even country castles to run training courses for their staff. Courses cover all sorts of topics: induction to the organization, specific job-related or people skills (assertiveness, negotiation) and developmental workshops aimed at middle or senior management.

But training is vulnerable to many factors: economic downturns mean that training budgets look easy targets for cuts; product and technical innovations mean training has to respond to different needs; demographic changes in the internal (employees) and external (purchasing) customers mean programmes soon become redundant.

There is a certain irony in that trainers who talk so much about change have themselves to change so often. Some trainers are gullible to state of the art, flavour of the month, fashion. But there are some noticeable trends in management and business training in the nineties. Though not *all* are apparent in *all* organizations, at least seven themes seem noticeable.

● **Learning not Training** Training is about acquiring specific skills; learning is more concerned with general principles. Training is for the here and now; it is company specific; it is highly practical, even pragmatic. Learning has less immediate application and is designed to be more useful in various contexts. Companies have preferred training because it is believed to be more cost-effective. Many firms don't believe it is their task to provide a rather general university-based education. That, they have argued, is a luxury which managers can buy for themselves, but more and more companies see the benefit in the well-educated manager, the intelligent generalist. Because there is nothing as practical as good theory they send their people off to acquire MBAs, or on longer developmental courses. The opportunity for learning (as opposed to training) may actually help staff retention in these firms and might even encourage better applicants. Learning is meant to generalize; it is about how to think and analyse problems; it is about where to look for a solution. Training is about acquisition of highly specific skills. University education is about learning; that is why it is valued.

● **Less Provincial, Chauvinistic, Ethnocentric Perspectives** We now have a global market, an international work force and multinational products. Management has had to take this into consideration. Cosy 'we-they' stories, case histories from local companies and a homogeneous work force

46

are a thing of the past. All managers need to take a wider perspective — not just pan-European, but global. Hence the focus on cultural differences, and comprehensive briefings on how other companies in other countries do things. The 'little Englander' trainer, like the vulgar American consultant, is facing extinction which inpart accounts for all the 'cross-cultural'; 'multinational'; 'across-boundaries' courses available. And whereas before a multi-coloured, multi-ethnic course presented problems (of tradition), now it is perceived as an asset, even an opportunity.

● **Competency-led Training** Despite the vagueness of the concept of competency, many organizations have been forced to think through exactly which competencies (skills, abilities, traits) they require of their managers. Having done this, they are frequently much more focused on what sort of training they need. In the past trainers provided what *they* thought appropriate, or more prosaically what they could offer. Now they are being required to integrate the training programme into the company's overall competence-led training, or human resource strategy. Courses that don't fit may be jettisoned, while others have to be created to meet the needs of the proposed strategy. Not all organizations have gone down the competency route, but the approach is becoming increasingly popular. A problem of this approach is that businesses may identify competencies for which no courses are available.

● **Team-building rather than Leadership** If the eighties were the *me* decade and the nineties are the *we* decade, how is this reflected in management training? Nearly everyone works in groups and business success is dependent not on individuals but teams. It really is true that a chain is only as strong as its weakest link. Recent research has stressed the importance of talented heterogeneous teams: teams with overall ability but whose members each had different skills, preferences, and approaches that *complemented* each other. Just as people may have to be trained to become leaders, they may also have to be trained to be followers. Training programmes now focus on how to build, sustain and manage a team; how to assess your favourite and most comfortable role when operating in a team; how to select individuals with a team in mind and how to be a better team member. Of course in places like Japan, where the collectivist nature of the society means that people grow up and always function in teams, they need the opposite of team-building, learning how to function as an individual and learning to praise individualism.

● **Virtual-reality Training** Trainers have always worried about the generalizability of training; that is, whether what you learn on courses in comfortable hotels or cosy training centres actually gets applied, let alone remembered, in the real work setting. The more realistic or similar the train-

47

ing environment to the work environment, the less, by definition, there is a problem of generalization. Think how much airlines spend on simulators! Trainers too are now considering training in situ on the shop floor, in the executive office or in the sales room. Though this may cause some inconvenience or might even actually be dangerous to customers or equipment, it is thought worth it. But if it is not possible through video-tapes or other methods, training has tended to get more naturalistic, reflecting much more accurately the situation in which the work is done. Chalk-and-talk, classroom learning is on the way out.

● **Using Managers as Trainers** It is not only because of the expense of staffing a permanent training department or calling in egotistical consultants that there is a trend for managers to become trainers themselves. People rightly expect that managers can in some circumstances act as trainers, because they are the ones with the most relevant knowledge. Most managers have the time and the skill to become explicit trainers rather than simply people to be imitated, but they can do a very useful job. Indeed some people are calling for a change in job title so that 'supervisors' become 'coaches', reflecting what their job really should be.

● **Using Subordinate Feedback** Most managers are used to being appraised by their superiors and occasionally by their peers. Trainers, on the other hand, are used to being rated by their course attendees. Because it is your subordinates who know you best and have to live with the consequences of your particular style, it is arguably they who provide the most useful feedback to managers on how to improve their management skills. Many organizations are even considering using subordinate ratings, not only as a useful feedback technique in training, but also as a possible source of data for staff appraisals. More and more trainers now are using upward or 'bottom-up' feedback compared to the more traditional downward appraisal.

Training, like other aspects of organizational life, is open to fad and fashion. Hence during the course of the nineties, it is likely that the above trends themselves will change.

➤ There is a strong movement away from short-term classroom-based training courses. A major concern is that learning does not generalize across time or work situations.

➤ Thus, following from what we know about learning in general, courses are led by managers themselves in the actual work setting and based on the contribution and functioning of teams rather than individuals.

➤ Organizations now seek out specific training courses in line with their defined relevant competencies. In this sense, companies now decide on what they want and look for it rather than find out what is available and choose from it.

➤ Because so much business involves people from other cultures and nations, courses attempt to teach where differences lie, how to understand people from different perspectives and how to adapt one's productto the preference of others.

C. How to Socialize New Employees

Most organizations have some type of programme or procedure designed to help new employees orient themselves and adjust to their new jobs. Effective induction of new recruits lets them know what type of organization they have joined, and begins to socialise them into the new corporate culture of which they are now a part. It also lays the groundwork for orienting employees towards their new working environment so that they know what is expected of them. This introduction to the company can play a crucial role in setting employees off on the right foot, enabling them to give their best to the company and feel good about doing so.

While organizational socialization is a complex process with many interacting facets, it essentially involves the successful attainment of three major goals: (1) providing employees with the basic work skills and information needed for their jobs, (2) orienting them to the practices, policies, and procedures of the organization, (3) helping them adjust to membership in their new work groups. A number of general guidelines have been identified as helpful in reaching each of these goals.

In the *sink-or-swim* approach, recruits are simply placed in their new jobs, and learn what they need from practical experience. In *job rotation,* they work at several different jobs in succession, thus acquiring a broad range of skills useful in different contexts. finally, in full-time *training,* they participate in training programmes ranging from classroom instruction to detailed on-the-job training. Whatever form they take, training programmes should adopt the following principles in order to succeed:

● Determine precisely what skills and information individuals need for their jobs; do not assume that their previous experience or professional training has armed them with these skills or information.

● Provide individuals with feedback on their work, and a sense of accomplishment about their growing expertise.

● Tailor training programmes to the needs of specific jobs; general or generic training cannot be readily applied or transferred in many cases.

● Evaluate the success of training programmes on a regular basis; do not assume that they are succeeding.

Orientation programmes focus on helping individuals understand current organization practices, policies and procedures. Most are fairly short-term in scope, occupying a few hours or a single day. In order for such programmes to succeed, they should take account of the following principles:

● Avoid information overload. New employees cannot possibly absorb everything they need to know about the organization in a single day. This should be spread out over a longer period of time.

● Don't over-emphasize paperwork; it is impossible for individuals to gain an accurate overview of an organization and how it operates from a day spent filling out one form after another.

● Orientation sessions should avoid scare tactics in which new employees are warned that their chances of success are quite low or which focus too heavily on praising the organization and its current practices.

● Be certain that the information provided is relevant; it should also be provided on a need-to-know basis.

● Build in two-way communication so that new recruits do not merely receive information in a passive manner; they should have opportunities to raise questions and seek clarification.

Work groups are a primary source of help for new employees. The people around them are doing similar jobs, and are often happy to share their knowledge and expertise with newcomers. In addition, they can provide much needed social support and encouragement in those trying early days. It is crucial, therefore, that socialisation programmes assist individuals in becoming integrated into their new work units. The following principles are often helpful in this respect.

1 Socialization should occur, as much as possible, within the work group; disjunctive procedures conducted by people from outside the organization are often less effective.

2 Be careful to expose new recruits primarily to talented, supportive co-workers with positive attitudes toward the organization; avoid exposure to employees with less favourable attitudes or work habits.

3 Avoid segregating newcomers into their own work unit; this can amount to the blind leading the blind, and can foster the development of faulty perceptions and beliefs about the organization.

4 Tell new recruits how long they will be on probationary status, and when they will become fully-fledged members of the organization; this helps eliminate one important and unnecessary source of ambiguity and worry.

By following these principles, organizations can help their new employees navigate successfully through the many pitfalls of organizational entry and socialization. The result will be recruits who are able to assume full responsibility and membership more quickly than might otherwise be the case, and who will hold more positive attitudes towards the organization, its procedures, and their co-workers.

➤ Effective induction into an organization is key to laying the groundwork for orienting new employees into the organization.

➤ Some organizations simply throw employees in at the deep end, others implement a job rotation scheme, while others have a formal training programme.

➤ It is important that induction and early training programmes inform employees fully about the organization without overloading them.

➤ Organizational socialization should involve co-workers and strike a balance between formal training and on-the-job experience.

D. Assessment Centres

A key task organizations face is identifying talented persons, suited for management or leadership roles. Many techniques for accomplishing this task have been developed, but one of the most successful has been the use of assessment centres.

An assessment centre is not a 'centre' at all. It is used to describe a process by which an individual, or group of individuals, is assessed by a team of judges using a comprehensive and integrated series of techniques. At least one of these techniques should be a work sample test or simulate an exercise which more or less directly represents or recreates important elements of real job tasks.

Other techniques often include interviews and standardized pencil and paper tests of mental abilities, aptitudes and personality characteristics.

The rationale behind these assessment procedures is as follows: it is assumed that certain traits or characteristics are closely related to success as a manager. To the extent that this is so, careful assessment of these characteristics should prove useful in predicting an individual's potential for this role.

An assessment centre generally results in a written report which combines quantitative information, for example scores on tests and exercises, ratings on dimensions of performance, with a more qualitative, descriptive account of the individual's apparent strengths and weaknesses. Recommendations to arise from this process may include a decision to select or promote an individual, advice on career development or counselling, training needs and so on.

Assessment centres actually have a range of applications within organizations. They have principally been used to identify management potential or balance. They have been applied in connection with employee recruitment, selection of employees for special placements or production, and to guide career development.

Assessment centres are much more elaborate in scope than the techniques for measuring personality (or other individual differences). Typically, they require two or three days rather than one or two hours of an individual's time. During this period, the persons being assessed are asked to perform a wide range of tasks designed to simulate conditions and activities they might encounter in their current or future jobs.

Assessment centres originated in Europe and can be traced back to multiple assessment procedures developed for officer selection in pre-war Germany. The general pattern of these procedures was that candidates were assessed over three days by a board consisting of a colonel, a medical officer and psychological examiners. The assessment also included a biographical interview, leadership tests, personality assessment, and participation in a group discussion. These German exercises inspired the British War Office Selection Board to adopt similar practices in selecting officers to the armed forces. The WOSB used a combination of observational techniques, lectures, obstacle courses, command situation simulations, pencil and paper tests, biographical questionnaires, peer assessments and interviews.

During the post-World War Two period, assessment centre development was continued further by the British Civil Service Selection Board. More emphasis was placed on paper work and tests of intellectual capacity by the civil service than upon physical aptitude. The CSSB assessed candidates in groups of seven at a residential centre over a forty eight hour period. The assessors were two administrative civil servants and a psychologist. Techniques used comprised a battery of mental ability and aptitude tests, questionnaires on interests and leisure pursuits, projective tests, peer assessments, interviews of each candidate by each assessor and situational tests. These exercises were evidently found to be highly predictive of future job performance.

Another example, of an assessment centre is the one used for many years by US telecommunications corporation AT&T, requiring two days of testing and includes an 'in-basket' exercise (in which individuals must deal with a number of memos, letters, and other items that might normally appear on a manager's desk each day), leaderless group discussions, simulated interviews, paper and pencil tests, and various management games or simulations.

Another key aspect of assessment centres is their emphasis on a number of different characteristics. Information relating to administrative skills, work motivation, social skills, creativity, maturity, independence, and many other traits is gathered. In some cases, the individuals who conduct such assessments are specially trained professionals. In other cases, they are people highly experienced in the tasks and jobs involved (practising managers). In many assessment centres, several raters assess each participant and then discuss their reactions until they reach a consensus. Regardless of such differences, all assessment centres involve efforts to measure a number of work-related characteristics through a wide range of tasks and careful observations by several different raters.

Research has indicated that, in general, assessment centres are useful: the information they provide is helpful in predicting management potential, future performance, and other important outcomes. However, assessment centres have not been found equally valid for all purposes. They appear to be most successful when used for early identification of managerial talent, but least successful when used to determine which individuals should be promoted. Further, they may be more successful in predicting future potential than in predicting ratings of current job performance. finally, assessment centres seem to be most successful when trained professionals (e.g., experts on personality testing) rather than co-workers or supervisors serve as assessors, and when several evaluation devices are used.

Setting up an assessment centre needs careful thought if it is to yield useful and effective results. There are several important steps to bear in mind.

● A systematic analysis of the job(s) for which one is selecting should be carried out with the aim of identifying the most important or critical elements.

● A set of carefully designed and chosen assessment techniques is needed, which are as far as possible representative of the more important job tasks and the competencies needed to perform those tasks.

● Simulation design requires particular attention. Simulations should directly represent real job situations, but the content should not be such as to give unfair advantage to candidates with detailed specialized knowledge.

● Assessor training is required to ensure that assessors are competent in behaviour observation and are working to a common standard.

Nowadays, most assessment centres make up some overall list of dimensions on which the performance of candidates is rated on dimensions after each exercise, and also at the end of the assessment centre as a whole. In other assessment centres, rating of dimensions is left until the end of the assessment procedures, after all information on candidates has been collected. There is no solid evidence on whether one approach is better than the other.

It is critical, however, that the dimensions are job-related, clearly defined and preferably illustrated with examples of relevant behaviour that might be observed during the assessment process. Well-designed dimensions of this kind give assessors a framework which guides their attention to important points of evidence and proves a common basis for discussion. Without dimensions, or the clear criteria to be applied, assessors may find themselves disagreeing not about assessees' performances but about the aspects of performance which they think are important.

While dimensions can be useful, there are potential pitfalls. These can generally be avoided, if dimensions are viewed as a means of examining candidates' performances rather than as ends in themselves. The main mistake is to interpret assessment centre dimensions as measures of stable and enduring personality-type traits.

Ratings of candidates on the same dimensions can vary considerably in different exercises. Consequently, conclusions about individuals are likely to be more valid if related to tasks and situations than if related only to dimensions.

Assessment centres can be a useful tool, yielding important practical benefits. They are not, however, an unmixed blessing. They are very costly to conduct, and negative ratings, if revealed to participants, can undermine their confidence, and hence their value to their organization. Still, assessment centres appear to represent a potentially valuable technique for measuring important differences between individuals and for choosing those persons most suited for increased management responsibility.

➤ Assessment centres are an approach to measuring personality and skills based on the ratings of individual's behaviour in wide range of tasks performed over a two or three day period.

➤ They are therefore expensive to run but tend to provide reliable information on candidate's ability.

➤ Although they may help identify various characteristics of candidates they cannot, of necessity, guarantee that those characteristics predict occupational success.

E. Training in the Great Outdoors

Does getting wet, cold and generally miserable in the countryside help you become a better manager? How can the use of boy-scout skills have anything to do with modern management? Isn't outdoor training just a way of keeping ageing PE teachers, sadistic ex-corporals and overpaid consultants gainfully employed? Is outward-bound training just an expensive fad in training, no better or worse than classroom teaching?

Cynics who are often against any sort of training want proof of its success, often in the form of some cost-benefit formula. And finding none, or at least nothing that really satisfies them, they reject the whole notion of outdoor training. Sceptics, on the other hand, argue that the more realistic the training in terms of what, where, and how you learn skills, the more effective it is. And because outward bound is hardly a simulation of business life, it can't really work.

So what is the philosophy of outdoor training? To a large extent, the answer depends on what traditional classroom or on-the-job training does not do. Essentially there are three good arguments:

● **Experimental vs Theoretical Learning** Since the sixties when 'EST' groups thrived, many trainers have pointed out that *real* learning occurs when people are put into difficult, novel, problematic situations. People have to be shocked out of their complacency to really learn about themselves and others. In trainer jargon, '*unfreezing*' needs to take place before real learning occurs. Learning occurs whilst people deal with these novel situations: not before with the study of elaborate theories or abstract ideas; and not afterwards, with bland debriefing. The philosophy of outdoor training is that people learn most about themselves, their teams, and their limitations, by *doing*. 'No gain without pain', and the pain is not the cold, damp, and discomfort, but rather dealing with performance issues in an unfamiliar setting.

● **Emotions not Ideas** Most training courses are about ideas, concepts, skills, and models. They involve brain work and traditional classroom activities. But as outdoor trainers tell you, management in a tough world is about self-confidence and courage. Most training aims at the head but not the heart. Anyone who has been on an outdoor training course will tell you immediately about the whole gamut of emotions they experience: pure blind fear; incredible fury and anger; maudlin depression and self-doubt; and unexpected tension-releasing humour. A major aim of outdoor training is to teach people that when pushed to the limit of their ability, they *can* do it. The great Victorian virtues of self-reliance, fortitude, even stoicism can be, and need to be, learned to be a successful manager. This does not take place with the cold learning experience of the classroom, but the white-hot experience of physical danger. Outdoor training is unashamedly about emotional learning.

● **Team-membership not Leadership** There are plenty of leadership courses but not too many on 'followership'. Despite mouthing platitudes to the contrary about teams and team work, Anglo-Americans come from an individualistic not a collective culture. Team work does not come easily or naturally. Hence it is more attractive to be the leader, because in that role you can more easily impose your individualistic style and preference on others. Learning to sail a yacht in choppy seas or cross a gorge via a pulley, sling and ropes necessitates real co-operation. Teams in the bush need to be inter dependent: you need them and they need you. You cannot survive on your own. And at times, the leader needs to be a follower and vice versa.

All people need to learn how to be an effective member of a team to exploit their assets, give of their expertise and to draw out the abilities and skills of others. This is rarely learned in intellectual problem-solving in the class-room, making paper models or being video-taped. The real team involve-ment in these situations is pretty minor, but that is definitely not the case on some outdoor courses.

Of course, not all outdoor training provides all the benefits. And certainly outdoor training is not *always* appropriate. Indeed, it can happen that it backfires in interesting and unusual ways. Rather than gaining self-confi-dence, some people can and do experience nothing but self-doubt. They can on occasion return broken, not built up. Others, discovering new-found strengths and abilities, pack up and go on to other organizations believing they would do better elsewhere.

The problem, of course, lies in measuring the effectiveness of training. How can one show conclusively that the time and money spent on outward-bound or similar courses is well spent? This is a fiendishly difficult question because although one can easily think of a number of possible measures nearly all have particular problems. But more importantly perhaps outdoor, or any other training, is unlikely to succeed in its aim if the organization is not prepared to change some of the contingencies that lead people to behave in such a way in the first place.

This is a paradox of all training. If a risk-averse organization chooses to send its managers rewarded for caution and prudence, on a course to stimu-late them to be more brave and adventuresome, but then punishes or ig-nores the very behaviour they learn on the course, it is no wonder the course is seen as a waste of time. Indeed this sort of behaviour might lead participants to becoming increasingly job dissatisfied and leave the organization!

Outdoor training is neither a panacea nor a total waste of time. If, as a client, you know what you want and what a good course can offer, you may be able to provide for your employees an enriching, even invaluable experience that will fundamentally change them in ways you find desirable. A bad course with no planned outcomes may result in increased employee cynicism, colds and scratches, or even worse, a badly bruised and critically injured ego. It should not be dismissed as nonsense nor embraced as the only solution. Chosen judiciously, and run well, outward-bound training can provide a unique learning experience.

➤ Outdoor, outward-bound training courses have existed since the 1940's and were virtually all aimed at sailors who might have to endure considerable hardship in a life boat.

➤ More recently sedentary businessmen have been sent on similar, if not modified and less strenuous, courses to develop their self-confidence and courage.

➤ While on these outward-bound type courses and shortly thereafter, peoples' belief about themselves, faith in their team and risk aversion do change.

➤ There remain doubts, however, as to whether these courses have any long term advantages, particularly if the organization from which individuals are sent does not embrace the adventurous and self-sufficient philosophy of the course itself.

F. Back to School:
Training Adults and Teaching Children

University lecturers teach the academic discipline of psychology through traditional lectures, practicals and tutorials, and management trainers train adults in what is loosely called management skills through lectures and exercises. The differences between the two should not be, but are, enormous. How much are these two seemingly similar enterprises alike or different?

It is not so much the fact that students tend to be young and immature and adults less so, or that students tend to be taught in institutions (like universities and colleges), because adults are also taught in institutions (namely business premises or hotels), but rather that the philosophy and feel of the two enterprises are so different.

The basic differences between them lie in the spirit and aim of the two enterprises. These are nicely reflected in the difference between the terms 'teach' and 'train'. For most academic courses, students are taught theory, first principles and abstract understanding. Their often unworldly dons are concerned that they understand the background and the theory behind what they are learning, be it anthropology or anatomy, physics or physiology, education or economics. The learning is frequently abstract without any obvious purpose except to deepen understanding.

For managers, on the other hand, the training in a particular topic is nearly always practical and concrete. The gritty, sensibleness of most of the courses echo a 'cut-the-crap' utilitarianism. Background details, historical origins, and theoretical models get rapidly jettisoned in favour of practical understanding and 'doing' skills. 'Training effectiveness' is defined as the speed by which people can acquire and practice relevant skills, not the extent to which they understand theoretical concepts.

Teaching students, even in applied courses, remains context-independent in the sense that they are rarely taught for a specific place, time or operation. Doctors, dentists, accountants, even lawyers are taught their subjects with the knowledge that they may take their skills and practice in a multitude of contexts. Hence abstract concepts are more useful; they cross boundaries easily. But management training, particularly if it is organizationally sponsored, is highly context-specific. Adults are trained in the house style, using the unique house concepts and language. Curiously it is frequently a source of pride to organisations that training is so context-specific: they believe it provides a source of unity, is highly efficient and the degree to which it can be applied elsewhere is irrelevant. Anyway, organizations don't feel they should do the training for other businesses, for fear that employees would use them as cheap sources of excellent training.

TEACHING STUDENTS		TRAINING MANAGERS
Theoretical/Abstract	PHILOSOPHY	Practical/Concrete
Understanding	AIM	Doing
Context-Independent	CONTEXT	Context-Specific
Long term, unlimited	TIME-FRAME	Short-term, immediate
Self-initiated	RESOURCES	Provided
Critical/Sceptical	TONE	Enthusiastic/Zealous
Verbal/Processes	MEDIUM	Diagrammatic/Models
Content	VALUES	Style

The time frame not only of the teaching but of the contents may differ. Academics tend to take a longer view of things. They are unused to being rushed, know few time-deadlines and are hence very tolerant of students who fail to get work done on time. Great work takes time; ideas have to mature. Time-to-completion is rarely a measure, except by default in examinations. This stands in very sharp contrast to the time-obsessed manager, newly returned from a 'just-in-time' lecture. Managers tell you that they live in flux and the world is a capricious, ever-changing place. Hence the shelf life of ideas and methods is short and thus training must be for the here and now. Therefore, the quicker the skills or ideas are obtained the better. Trainers use topical examples, are conscious of fashion and like to boast about being up to date, state of the art users of both ideas and technology.

Students are given reading lists, library cards and shown where the laboratory, computer and language centre are. They are then expected to be disciplined, inner-directed and self-initiated. Facilities and resources are provided minimally, but students are expected to be enterprising, self-starters who seek out more or better resources. A friend of the first author's from a management training school once described her one year university postgraduate course as the most expensive reading list in the world! Management and in-house trainees do expect and receive all the literature and materials they need for the topic because time is short, and it is considered the job of the trainers to compile. This is one reason that in-house adult training is so expensive. Sophisticated materials and up-to-date technology are available for the trained, not the taught!

Academics are cautious, critical, sceptical sort of people. They use the word 'perhaps' a lot; papers are entitled 'Towards an understanding of ...' They take a long time to be convinced of things and are trained to be questioning and doubting. This tone is reflected in the teaching: students have literary criticism; managers literary appreciation. Only theologians are taught apologetics; others get criticism. Students are encouraged to be like their dons: intellectually phlegmatic, muted in their enthusiasm. Trainers, on the other hand, are rewarded for, and reward themselves, high levels of enthusiasm and certainty. Their models, the 'gurus', know the answers, are certain about the solution, believe in the theory. They persuade by personal conviction, much like a religious converter. Indeed, training is evangelical: it is frequently made out to be fun and its benefits are praised. Criticism, positive or negative, is not encouraged and, indeed, these two very different types of critique are frequently confused.

Teaching students is a verbal process. That is not to say that diagrammatic models, formulae, and charts are not used but rather they are more frequently used to summarize and illustrate. Academics try to understand the process or mechanism which may or may not be easily open to illustration. Bullet points may be used but again mainly as shorthand. But the medium, like the message, is verbal and abstract, too complex and subtle for easily comprehensible slides.

Trainers, on the other hand, are often highly reliant on elaborate, often multi-coloured slides, frequently with various boxes, connected by lines. How and why things are categorized or boxed in a particular way is rarely spelt out. Models or charts are used to simplify, categorize, render easily memorable. Sometimes amusing terms are used to facilitate memory and because trainers know that post-course evaluation scores are closely examined they try hard to amuse.

Pilots talk of bad flying as all thrust and no rudder, and driving instructors of bad pupils as all accelerator and no gears. By this they attempt to distinguish between the expert and the novice. Another occasionally used pejorative remark, not unrelated to the above, is all style and no content. Often academic lectures may contain excellent content delivered in a dry, unappealing, indeed even off-putting lecturing style. A monotonous delivery with no pacing or light-and-shade is frequently the lot of the undergraduate. Competent, sometimes brilliant content, spoilt by unsophisticated delivery and presentation style.

By contrast some management trainers demonstrate a polished, modern, sophisticated style. Slides, videos, even role-plays are carefully prepared, and thoughtfully ordered. There is variety, amusing context and a good pace. But frequently the content or the substance suffers at the hands of the liturgy. Just as the popular (tabloid) media attempt attractive presentation at the cost of sophistication of ideas, and the broad-sheets good analysis in favour of easy reading, so the trainer prefers access and the teacher comprehensiveness.

In short, at university students learn the process of learning and argument as much as the subject matter. The very essence of university education is that it provides a set of abstract rules and understanding that can be applied to many situations. But all this applies to present day Britain. American universities, more market sensitive than our own, tend to be more in the management training tradition described above.

Readers from both sides of this divide will no doubt strongly object to this 'compare and contrast' exercise, claiming how mislabelled they have been. Frequently when a distinction is made one pole or type is more attractive than the other and neither side will happily accept what they see as a slur on their educational activities.

But in our experience the movement from one world to the other is neither common nor easy. The corduroyed don may not so easily be able to supplement his meagre stipend at training courses. Equally the pin striped trainer may not easily acquire the cachet he or she hopes by teaching at the local university. The skills, style and outlook of these two activities sometimes clash dramatically and one is forced to take sides. And, like the lay conception of schizophrenics, one can be in two minds about who is right.

➤ Training courses aim at providing people with specific concepts or skills. Training course pupils expect, and get, all materials and expect, through their lively teachers, to become competent in a skill in a short period.

➤ Trainers are sensitive to their pupil clients and may be rated by them. Indeed the fact that they are rated after each course, and kept on as a function of the ratings, may have a lot to do with their style.

➤ University and college teachers have longer-term objectives. They are less interested in skills, save perhaps that of learning itself, but also debate, writing and critical analysis. They are less market sensitive, often to the point of being inadequate teachers.

➤ The trainer could learn from the don the importance of teaching abstract thinking that renders students more able to help themselves, while the university lecturer might benefit from learning how to teach more appealingly to their long-suffering listeners.

G. Mentors

In many fields, young and inexperienced individuals learn from older, more experienced ones. Thus, in medicine and law, interns learn much from established physicians and attorneys; and in science, graduate students acquire a broad range of knowledge and skills from established researchers under whose guidance they work. Does the same process of *mentorship* operate in business settings? A growing body of evidence suggests that it does. Young and relatively inexperienced employees often report that they have learned a great deal from a mentor — an older and more experienced employee who advises, counsels, and otherwise enhances their personal development.

These days mentoring has become a more formalised area of management development. A survey by the Industrial Society has indicated that forty per cent of British companies have a mentoring scheme and a further twenty per cent are thinking about one.

Research on the nature of such relationships suggests that mentors do many things for their protégés. Put simply, a mentor is someone with experience who offers help and knowledge to someone junior. The mentor is not the boss, nor is he or she trying to teach something specific. Mentors provide much needed emotional support and confidence. They advance the protégé's career by nominating him or her for promotions, and by providing opportunities for the protégé to demonstrate his or her competence. They suggest useful strategies for achieving work objectives one's protégés may not generate for themselves. They bring the protégé to the attention of top management, a necessary first step for advancement. finally, they protect protégés from the repercussions of errors, and help them avoid situations that may be risky for their careers.

Research in the United States has shown that mentoring can be beneficial, with top executives who had had a mentor doing better than those who had not.

In the 1980's mentoring caught on in the UK as a way of helping graduates settle down in big companies. Now there are mentors for managers at all levels, mentors for disadvantaged groups of employees and even mentors for mentors.

The idea accords well with the latest management thinking whereby employees 'own' their development and in flat organizations, where people are no longer being told what to do by their immediate superiors, they need others to guide and help them.

Of course, the potential gains are offset by possible risks or hazards. Protégés who hitch their wagon to a falling rather than a rising star may find their own careers in danger when their mentors suffer setbacks. Indeed, in some cases they may find themselves without a job if a purge follows defeat in a political struggle. In addition, mentors are only human, so not all the advice they supply is helpful. And there is always the danger that protégés will become so dependent upon their mentors that their development as self-reliant individuals able to accept authority and responsibility is slowed.

Many early US efforts went wrong because they were too formal and they established so many rules for the behaviour of mentors and mentorees that the relationship was stifled. In the UK, the problem seems to be a lack of structure and agreed direction to the mentoring relationship. Those giving and receiving mentoring need to prepare properly, get clear their goals for the scheme and the relationship, and support from the company is needed to ensure problems don't arise.

Mentors themselves are not totally selfless benefactors who never want anything in return. On the contrary, they expect several things from protégés. first, they expect their protégés to turn in hard work and effort on assigned tasks. Secondly, they expect them to be loyal supporters within the organization; after all, they are now members of the mentor's team. Thirdly, mentors may gain recognition from others in the company for helping to nurture young talent, and can bask in the reflected glory of any success gained by their protégés. finally, they may reap psychological benefits from feeling needed, and from a sense of accomplishment in helping the younger generation.

Other findings suggest that mentor-protégé pairs do not form at random. Mentors are usually older than their protégés (by about eight to fifteen years). They tend to be people with considerable power and status within their companies. As a result, they are able to assist rising young stars without feeling threatened.

How do mentors select their protégés? Existing evidence suggests that they may begin by noticing and being impressed by a young employee's initial performance, or find interacting with them easy and pleasant. This may be because mentor and protégé share similar attitudes and backgrounds, or because protégés are socially skilled and clearly transmit their desire for an experienced tutor. In still other cases, would-be protégés approach potential mentors and actively ask for help or attempt to initiate a relationship in other ways.

Most human relationships develop over time and mentorship is no exception to this general rule. In fact, most mentor-protégé relationships seem to pass through several distinct phases. The first, known as *initiation*, can last from six months to a year and represents a 'courtship' period during which the relationship gets started and takes on importance for both parties. The second phase, known as *cultivation*, may last from two to five years. During this time, the bond between mentor and protégé deepens, and the young individual may make rapid career strides because of the skilled assistance he or she is receiving. The third stage, *separation*, begins when the protégé feels it is time to assert independence and strike out on his or her own, or when there is some externally produced change in the role relationships (e.g., the protégé is promoted; the mentor is transferred). Separation can also occur if the mentor feels unable to continue providing support and guidance to the protégé (e.g., if the mentor is experiencing physical illness or psychological problems). This phase can be quite stressful in cases where the mentor resents the protégé's growing independence, or in instances where the protégé feels that the mentor has withdrawn support and guidance prematurely. If separation is successful, the relationship may enter a final stage termed *redefinition*. Here, both individuals perceive their bond primarily as one of friendship. They come to treat one another as equals, and the roles of mentor and protégé may fade away completely. However, the mentor may continue to take pride in the accomplishments of the former protégé, while the latter may continue to feel a debt of gratitude toward the former mentor.

Recent evidence suggests that some of the early claims for the powerful benefits of mentorship were probably overstated. Nevertheless, having an experienced, powerful mentor does seem helpful in many situations, and gives at least some young people an important edge. Unfortunately, this conclusion has unsettling implications for women, who often seem to have less access to suitable mentors than men. Several factors contribute to this state of affairs. first, there are simply fewer senior female executives available to serve as mentors for young female employees. Secondly, women have fewer interactions with people in positions of power in many organizations. As a result, they are less plugged into informal networks, and less likely to obtain a mentor. Thirdly, women are becoming more visible in many organizations. This may cause at least some potential mentors to feel reluctant to adopt this role; after all, if a female protégé is unsuccessful, her failure will receive more attention and reflect on the mentor to a greater extent than might be the case with a male protégé. Fourthly, many potential male mentors are reluctant to adopt this role because of concern over misinterpretation of the relationship. They realise that their interest in and concern for a younger female employee may well be misinterpreted by others, and this may pose a danger to their own careers.

➤ Young, inexperienced individuals can learn a great deal from older, established professionals. Mentoring may play a key role in employee development.

➤ Mentors can provide occupational and emotional support for their protégés, and create opportunities for career progression.

➤ The downside of this relationship is that protégés may suffer if their mentor falls on hard times.

➤ Eventually, both parties must be prepared to allow their relationship to mature to a point where the protégé achieves independence and may even supersede the mentor.

H. The Effectiveness of Television and Video in Business Training

A number of changes are coming together to make the 1990's the age of business television. Several powerful new technologies have emerged which make it possible to communicate electronically in ways that few had thought about during the 1980's. Television has evolved into a two-way communication medium through the use of satellite, computing and telecommunications technologies. It has developed a new and advanced flexibility which has opened up applications within business and industry which go far beyond its traditional form as a uni-directional transmitter of information.

Managers all over the advanced world are realising that one of the most important ingredients for business success in the future will be communication. With increased globalization of business organization, and growing costs of business travel, face to face meetings may not always be convenient or cost-effective. Instead, new forms of communication which can provide immediacy of contact for parties in different locations could be the solution, especially where they can see as well as hear each other.

With increasingly competitive marketplaces, speed of decision making is essential. This in turn needs to be fed by rapid and effective forms of communication. It is not only in the realm of doing business that rapid communications are needed. Organizations need skilled employees. Personnel training can take time. More and more, however, companies cannot wait several years for a corporate training scheme to cascade down through the organization. They may need to train or increasingly re-train employees over much shorter time spans in order to remain competitive and retain market share. It is frequently impossible to do that with people alone; there has to be a technological way of delivering training programmes quickly and accurately to large numbers of employees. Television and related audio-visual technologies can play a vital role in facilitating such a training process.

These are the needs which the business community has. In Europe the realization that television can help to satisfy these needs has been slow in coming for a mixture of cultural, technical and legal reasons. With increased pressure for change in the business world, these barriers are being dismantled and greater attention is being devoted to the use of television and video communications in the business context.

During the early decades of television, it was used and considered only as a one-way mass communication medium. During the 1980's the video cassette burst on to the scene. This meant that television programmes could be captured, packaged and sold as products. It afforded greater control to the receivers of television material. Programmes could be shown to target audiences at times chosen by the viewer not the broadcaster. This important technological development opened up new applications for television which came to be seen as more than just an entertainment medium.

Among these new applications were ones which were conceived potentially to be of benefit to the business community. Television and video provided new corporate communications channels which could be utilised by organizations to reach customers, suppliers and employees.

The business potential of television and video was not perceived straight away. Managers moved towards these new business technologies cautiously at first, but then as confidence grew, applications became more adventurous. Further, a new industry was spawned. Video production houses began to emerge to meet the demand for corporate videos which were the television equivalent of printed brochures and annual reports. Very large companies installed their own studios and film units to make their own programmes.

Business television and video communications are now used by many large organizations to convey business-related information within the company, for staff training, to carry intra-organizational promotions and marketing messages, and for tele-conferencing. The last of these applications is particularly attractive for international corporations and can facilitate meetings among personnel situated in diverse corners of the globe.

The production of television is a highly specialized profession which requires trained personnel who understand the grammar of the medium. The key to success in producing effective television programmes lies not simply in knowing about production techniques, but in understanding the audience. In broadcast television which goes out to many millions of people, programmes will provide different gratifications for and elicit different reactions from different viewers.

With business television, the aims are generally much more specific and the prime objective is to communicate a key message accurately and consistently to a clearly defined target group. It is important that the maker of business programmes, whether they are produced for delivering corporate messages to employees or for staff training purposes, should understand his or her target audience and how they are likely to respond to programmes made for them.

It is all too often the case, however, that programme makers produce programmes to impress other programme makers rather than to achieve the desired result among targeted viewers. Measuring the effectiveness of programmes, particularly those designed to deliver specific kinds of information or knowledge to special audiences, is a highly skilled operation in itself, requiring appropriate and systematic research techniques.

It is important that a business programme starts out with a clear objective and clearly defined message which it wants to get across. It is essential to understand the motivations and needs of the audience to know how they are likely to respond to a particular message. In addition, it is important to understand the capabilities of viewers in respect of being able to process information presented in a television programme. Production techniques can either help or hinder the information process. Using the wrong techniques may render an important training programme ineffective.

It is well established with broadcast news, for instance, that viewers may forget ninety per cent of the programme within a matter of hours. Level of audience interest in the subject is important of course. But even attentive viewers may fail to retain most of the programme as a result of information overload or distracting presentational features which interfere with effective learning of central story ingredients.

Thus, systematic measurement of audience response to business programmes is vitally important as an objective check on whether they have achieved what they were designed for. Objective assessment of business programme effectiveness needs to be stressed. This may mean going beyond simply asking viewers whether they felt that the programme had worked and been of benefit to them. In addition, it might be important to measure just how much they actually did learn or remember from it.

By linking this assessment directly to programme features such as use of visual images and illustrations (i.e., moving film, still photographs, charts, graphics and schematic drawings), narrative structure, content organization, camera angles, presenters, studio layout and so on, needed adjustments can be pinpointed to ensure more effective communication next time around.

It is important to understand what television is good at. This means acknowledging the fact that television (and video) can be effective in getting across to an audience certain types of information, but may be less effective on their own at communicating other types of information.

US reseach has claimed that a message learnt throught video is forty per cent more likely to be retained than one taught through chalk and talk, but the effectiveness of electronic audio-visual communications can fluctuate widely depending upon the appropriateness of the production techniques to the tuition context.

In the training context, television may be able to illustrate points in a way no other form of communication can match. It can also reach far more individuals with a single broadcast than a live lecture. Even so, the pace at which information is presented in a programme may be difficult for some (or even many) viewers to cope with. Furthermore, when a narrative is simultane-

70

ously illustrated by pictures, unless the information presented through these two channels is mutually reinforcing, information uptake by the audience members may be severely impeded.

The need to get the programme right is underpinned by cost considerations. The production process in itself may be costly. In addition the corporate issues with which the programme deals are generally going to be of the utmost importance, with significant implications for the organization's functioning and competitiveness. There is an important need to ensure that business television and video material works. This requires appropriate forms of audience research to assess the performance of the production process.

> ➤ New audio-visual technologies can be used to facilitate the rapid dispensation of training and other communications around organizations, even when employees are based in geographically distant sites.
>
> ➤ Audio-visual media developments have meant that they no longer provide only a one-way flow of information. Interactive media technologies now mean that employees can be message senders as well as receivers.
>
> ➤ It is important that television and video are more than just cosmetics. The successful and effective use of these forms of communication depend on a proper understanding of how they operate and how audiences respond to the messages they send.
>
> ➤ The production of television programmes for training must be driven by a thorough knowledge of audience needs and information processing capabilities.

3
PERFORMANCE ASSESSMENT

Whether they like it or not most managers are required to evaluate the performance of their staff on a regular basis. Some organizations have an elaborate, sophisticated performance management system that requires much form-filling and computer analysis.

This section explores some of the many issues currently hotly debated in the whole area of performance appraisal — the problems of using rating scales; performance-related pay; and upward (as opposed to downward) appraisal.

Nothing provokes quite so much passion as the issue of assessment. Cynics argue that poor performers advocate equality, promotion by seniority and no appraisal, while good performers prefer equity, promotion by ability and appraisal to satisfy their own ends.

EXECUTIVE CAR PARK

A. Rate as you would be Rated

Customer satisfaction surveys and rating forms for people at work are now in widespread use. Hotels, airlines, restaurants, even churches provide their customers with cards and forms asking them to rate service, products and personnel. Not many people choose to tick the boxes and give institutions the feedback they require. Indeed, some give little incentives — a free drink, even a cheap calculator — to encourage customers to comply and improve the response rate.

Most managers also have to provide an explicit evaluation of the performance of their subordinates at least annually, by completing an, albeit short, appraisal form. For some this is a bit like a school report with the most common phrases being satisfactory or adequate. Given widespread unpopularity of unstructured report writing, many organizations devise appraisal forms where boxes are ticked to indicate the quality of performance against various criteria.

Many managers are hostile or resistant to rating subordinates, precisely because they are supposed to offer objective, impartial evaluations. They know, all too well, the errors and injustices that can occur in the process. For those who don't already have these insights it is worth rehearsing them again here.

Perhaps the most common error is called the *halo* effect. It can be nicely illustrated by two examples. What most people are struck by when visiting a mental hospital is not that the inmates are dangerous or pretty obviously 'mad', but that they do tend to be ugly. It is pretty rare to find a physically attractive mental patient. The same is true of prisoners for similar reasons. When judges and psychiatrists decide on 'sentences', it seems they are influenced by the looks of the person. What is beautiful is good. And vice versa.

It is also not unknown for female secretaries and PAs to be selected more for their legs than their word-processing ability. All selection interviewees know that appearance may be as, if not more, important than ability in getting a job. Most attempt a positive halo by emphasising their best qualities, whatever they are.

A second cause of error and lack of objectivity lies in being too lenient or too harsh. This type of error is called *central tendency*. However long the rating form, and whatever its contents, some managers happily tick all the centre boxes and avoid the extremes. They do so because they do not want to over-praise an individual which might cause an inappropriate and unfulfillable rise in expectations for promotion, or salary increase. They also avoid the low scores because they want to avoid controversy over the appraisal and dealing with the anger, sulking and resentment of a poorly-rated subordinate. The net result is that everybody comes out as average and the whole exercise is a waste of time.

A third problem is memory, also called *recency bias*. Because managers rarely keep detailed notes, they do not remember the behaviours they have to rate. When workers score any major success, nobody remembers, but if they make one major cock-up, nobody forgets. Certainly most people rate the recent past no matter how representative it is.

Of course, another very common problem is *personal bias* and *prejudice*. This may be overt or covert, sophisticated or simple. We all have our preferences and prejudices based on past experience and it is often fairly difficult not to let these influence the ratings.

Thus, notwithstanding the quasi-scientific, and certainly numeric, feel of evaluation and appraisal forms, many managers complain that they are far from objective. They argue that there are so many sources of bias, like the few mentioned above, they are not only worthless but dangerous.

But this iconoclastic attitude doesn't take into account the fact that people can be taught to use the forms effectively. Coffee tasters, dog show judges, driving licence testers are all open to the above errors when they rate beans, animals or driving behaviour. But they learn to overcome them.

When it comes to managing people, it is crucial that they are appraised and given accurate, specific and comprehensive feedback. filling out forms encourages that and can be most helpful. Most managers would like their boss to provide them with detailed feedback but they all seem more hesitant about appraising their staff — often because they don't know how to conduct progress reviews with subordinates. So what do sceptics and cynics of rating forms want in their place? As our extremely active ex-Prime Minster used to shout in the Commons 'There is no alternative'.

➤ Most managers are required to produce an annual performance appraisal on subordinates. Often these reports are poorly structured and lack clear directives.

➤ Managers may feel uneasy about having to evaluate their staff. Moreover, appraisals may unfairly favour or disfavour particular employees in ways which have little to do with actual job performance.

➤ It is important that performance appraisals are accurate, objective and based on a systematic, factual account of how employees have behaved at work. If they are not, it is a sad testimony to ineffectual management and may jeopardise the future progression of employees.

B. Performance Appraisal

One of the most important processes in any organization is the evaluation of performance. *Performance appraisals* are crucial to effective personnel decisions, determining which employees should receive pay rises, promotions, bonuses, and other rewards and which ones, perhaps, should be downgraded or even dismissed. Ideally, performance appraisal should be a totally rational process, one in which completely objective evaluators use properly validated measures to assign ratings to individual employees.

Designing valid measures of performance is a complex matter. If they are to be useful, such measures should reflect *all* aspects of performance, but should *not* include unrelated or irrelevant behaviour. Similarly, such measures should be presented in a format that raters can easily understand and use.

In addition, human beings are far from perfect when called upon to evaluate others. They possess a limited capacity to process, store, and retrieve information. Further, their perceptions or interpretations of information relating to performance appear to be subject to many extraneous influences.

There is evidence that when the performance ratings for staff are radically different from managers' expectations, the manager may assign a higher or lower rating than the employee in fact warrants in order to make it consistent with anticipated performance. Thus, if an employee scores higher than expected he might actually be given a lower rating by his manager. Discovering that their predictions have failed can be a difficult pill for some managers to swallow.

This phenomenon was demonstrated in a study among supervisors in a large bank who were asked to indicate how well they expected their two newest tellers to do on the job. Then, four months later, they rated the actual performance of these individuals. Results indicated that when their expectations were disconfirmed, the supervisors rated the tellers lower than when these expectations were confirmed. In other words, these managers assigned lower ratings to tellers who performed either better or worse than they predicted than to tellers whose performance matched their earlier predictions.

These findings have unsettling implications, especially for individuals who expend extra effort on the job and do better than their supervisors expect. Apparently, such anticipated increments in performance may sometimes result in *lower* rather than higher performance appraisals.

Does this mean that employees are locked into whatever level of performance their managers expect? Not necessarily. Effects such as the ones just noted can be avoided if managers realise that their predictions failed simply because a new element entered the equation, such as increased motivation on the part of a subordinate.

How then can the accuracy of performance appraisals be improved? Performance appraisal is a serious business. Errors in this process can have important effects on both employees and the organizations who employ them. Promising careers can be shattered by unfair or inaccurate assessments. And organizations can experience major costs if undeserving individuals are rewarded and rise to positions they can't handle. Given these facts, efforts to make appraisals as accurate as possible seem well worthwhile.

One approach involves providing raters with special training experiences designed to help them overcome serious sources of error. A number of different procedures have been developed for this purpose. The most promising of these, however, appear to be those based largely on an *information-processing* approach to performance appraisal. According to this perspective, appraisal is a complex mental process in which raters must register and later recall as much information as possible about those being assessed. Then, they must use this information to evaluate those they have to rate in some manner. In order to improve appraisal accuracy, therefore, raters' ability to perform these tasks must be enhanced. Two techniques seem especially helpful in this regard.

The first of these is known as *frame of reference training*. As its name suggests, such training is designed primarily to establish a common frame of reference raters can use in evaluating performance. In this training, the work or tasks to be evaluated are described in detail and raters are given practice in using the rating instruments and scales they will employ. Detailed feedback on their accuracy in using these scales is also provided. Next, they are given clear explanations for the ratings assigned to various behaviours or levels of performance by expert raters. In sum, raters receive information on key dimensions of performance they are to evaluate, get practice in evaluating specific examples of performance, and receive feedback on their practice ratings. In this way, the links between performance dimensions and actual behaviour are clarified.

Growing evidence suggests that frame of reference training is quite successful. Individuals who receive it demonstrate less tendency toward halo effects and other forms of rating errors and greater accuracy than individuals who receive no training, or those who are simply informed about the nature of such errors. Frame of reference training seems to succeed, at least in part, because it induces raters to engage in what has been termed *deeper levels of processing* careful, detailed thought about raters' behaviour.

Two other techniques that are successful in improving the accuracy of performance appraisal are *training in observational skills* efforts to help raters become better observers of subordinates' behaviour (e.g. learning to take careful notes on their actions) and *decision training* helping raters understand the kind of inferential errors decision-makers often make when combining information about others. This training involves familiarizing raters with such potential errors as assigning inappropriate weights to various behaviours by subordinates, jumping to false conclusions about them, and ignoring the periods of biased data (e.g. inadequate samples of subordinates' behaviour). Both training in observational skills and decision training appear to reduce several types of errors while enhancing overall accuracy. Fortunately, these gains are attained after only a few hours of training.

Another important aspect of performance assessment is the appraisal interview. Many managers, however, report that providing feedback to subordinates in the context of a formal appraisal interview is one of the most difficult tasks they must perform. Unless such sessions turn into a 'love feast', they include at least some amount of negative feedback, and this is something most people are reluctant to deliver.

How can the potential unpleasantness of such sessions be minimized, and their value in improving employee motivation and performance be enhanced? There are no simple answers, but observing a few simple rules of thumb can help.

Do the following:

1 Agree, in advance, on the content of the interview exactly what issues will be discussed.

2 Agree on the process. How the interview will be conducted, what materials will be considered, and the sequence of these events.

3 During the interview, try to give feedback that is specific in nature and considerate in tone. General statements (e.g. 'You need to improve') aren't nearly as helpful as ones that focus on specific actions employees should take (e.g. 'You should fill in all R-20 reports on time').

4 Focus on the subordinate's behaviour, not on your inferences about the traits or characteristics it suggests. (This will help minimize the impact of such cognitive factors as implicit personality theories and stereotypes.)

5 Develop a concrete plan for improvement; one that outlines specific actions the subordinate can take to obtain higher evaluations next time.

6 Emphasize the fact that you are trying to help. Your goal is to help the subordinate improve, not to wreck his or her ego.

7 End by summarizing the major points, and with as much encouragement

as you can muster. Employees should leave feeling hopeful and capable of implementing the plan that has been developed.

Don't do the following:

1 Don't schedule the interview at a very busy time, or the end of the day; if you do, it will be hard to give it the attention it deserves.

2 Don't use threats (e.g. 'If you don't improve, you're through'). These usually generate negative, counterproductive reactions on the part of subordinates.

3 Don't compare the individual negatively to others ('If only you had handled it like so and so').

4 Don't attribute poor performance to stable internal causes (e.g. the employee's personality or lack of ability); if you can't attribute poor performance to temporary, external factors, leave this issue open.

5 Don't establish barriers to open communication (e.g. don't hold the interview in the supervisor's office if this is the only time the employee ever comes there; don't place physical barriers such as a desk between yourself and the person being appraised).

> ➤ Performance appraisals are crucial to effective personnel decisions.
>
> ➤ Valid measures of performance are vital.
>
> ➤ The accuracy of performance appraisals can be enhanced through frame of reference training and observational skills training.
>
> ➤ Appraisal interviews need to be conducted in a carefully planned and systematic fashion with appraiser and appraisee both being properly aware of the procedure and objectives.

C. Performance Related Pay

During the 1980's individual performance-related pay (PRP) took root in British service and manufacturing companies. With the publication of the Citizens' Charter underlining the government's determination to improve public services, such systems are likely to become more commonplace throughout the public sector.

Care is needed, however, among both public sector and private sector employers who may be thinking about PRP schemes for their own organization. The experience of some of those who have tried these schemes has revealed that they can have harmful consequences for staff morale unless properly introduced.

Even supporters of PRP have yet to convince sceptics that it has a direct effect on efficiency or productivity. Some personnel managers have found that these schemes can be expensive and have uncertain impact on employee motivation. Many organizations which converted to performance-related pay systems may have done so because it was fashionable. Serious questions are now being asked about how objective you can be in setting standards in many occupations and companies.

Despite these growing doubts, there is scant evidence of schemes being withdrawn. This may reinforce the view of PRP supporters that such schemes are robust and effective, or may simply reflect an unwillingness of organizations to give up in haste a system in which they have invested a great deal.

According to a 1992 survey by the National Economic Development Office and the Institute of Personnel Managers, forty seven per cent of private sector companies had PRP schemes for all non-manual grades and a further twenty one per cent were using it for some non-manuals. Not all of these schemes were recent developments; about one-third of those surveyed by NEDO/IPM were more than ten years old.

Among the attractions of performance-related pay is that, properly administered, it can be fairer than systems which reward employees merely for long service and assesses rewards on the basis of how well an employee has performed on the job.

Many employers also introduce PRP as one of a series of measures to change the culture in the workplace. Other changes include improved communications systems, profit sharing and company health schemes, all designed to make individuals associate themselves more closely with their employers.

Performance-related pay schemes can generate a negative backlash in some quarters. Trade unions tend to be suspicious of management's motives, often perceiving the real reason for the introduction of such schemes as being to weaken union power. Some independent research has corroborated this view, although it is uncertain as to how widespread such motivation really is.

Although union leaders have yet to be convinced, union memberships tend to be more accommodating. In organizations with PRP, the majority of employees tend to support the principle of it. Problems are more likely to arise, however, in the way such schemes are put into practice. Most employees who find themselves in performance-related pay schemes tend to doubt whether it improves the quality or quantity of their work. Nor do they tend to believe it makes them work harder. One particular area of doubt about the operation of PRP which can arise concerns perceived favouritism in the way performance assessments are made.

The failure of practice to live up to the standards anticipated from theory can result if insufficient thought is given to operational procedure. Once this perception is made by employees, PRP can do much more harm than good.

There are, however, steps that employers can take to safeguard against the serious damage an ill-fitted, poorly implemented PRP scheme can wreak in an organization.

first, a performance-related pay scheme works most effectively when properly integrated with other key organizational systems. The best schemes are those which are introduced with other human resource management techniques and in the context of a wider performance management system. Organizations with a performance management system generally have a shrewd vision of objectives, conduct formal reviews of progress towards targets and evaluate the effectiveness of the process.

Secondly, care should be taken with how money is allocated. One school of thought argues that performance-related pay should not be made too easy to obtain or be widely available to almost everyone. Instead a scheme works best when bonus payments are restricted only to the highest performers. Others believe that such restrictive practice is harmful to staff morale and motivation and that payments should be received by practically every employee. Some organizations have included quota systems to restrict the numbers of employees who are able to receive payments in any given year. This too can cause resentment because many employees could successfully achieve targets only to find they were rejected for a performance reward because too many colleagues had also achieved their targets.

In theory, successful performance-related pay schemes should be self-financing. Even so, organizations should be aware that in the first year or so they may incur extra costs in consultancy fees, training communications and, in some cases, buying the support of employees for the scheme against union opposition.

Thirdly, many organizations, upon introducing performance-related pay also want, as part of another fashionable trend, to encourage employees to work in teams. The two concepts sometimes clash with one another because PRP can, if employers are not careful, encourage employees to compete with one another. There are ways around this problem. Organizations can, for instance, divide employees into business units and encourage these units to identify team objectives where appropriate in assessing performance pay for managers.

Fourthly, there are important matters relating to discrimination which organizations must address on introducing performance-related pay. PRP runs on personal assessments of employees. There are particular dangers in discriminating between the sexes. The Equal Opportunities Commission says that even the most objective systems of performance-related pay and appraisal are likely to apply more readily to jobs performed by men than women.

Organizations guilty of discrimination risk not only alienating their female workforce, but also leaving themselves open to a challenge under European legislation.

> Performance-related pay is a growing phenomenon, but needs to be introduced and implemented with care.

> There remain question marks over whether PRP has a positive and direct effect on efficiency or productivity.

> There is a view that PRP is a fair method for rewarding employees, on the basis of how they have performed.

> PRP can create a negative backlash, particularly among unions who may see it as a power threat.

> Ineffectiveness may stem from poor implementation as much from the inability of PRP schemes per se to motivate employees.

> PRP schemes must be scrupulously fair in the way rewards are linked to performance; employers should not make rewards too easy to obtain, and such schemes should pay for themselves.

> Care is needed over the use of such schemes in relation to team performance, and avoidance of unfair discrimination towards certain types of employee must be studiously implemented.

D. Pay Equity

Odd things sometimes happen during office moving. Recently a group of American life insurance underwriters of varying degrees of seniority (ranging from underwriter trainees, associate underwriters to underwriters) were temporarily assigned (over a two week period) to the offices of one of their co-workers as their offices were being refurbished.

Some were assigned to the offices of a higher status persons, others were assigned to the offices of lower status persons, still others were assigned to the offices of equal status persons. finally, there was a non-movement group of underwriters who continued working in their own offices throughout the period. Over this fortnight a measure of productivity was made, taking into account the number of hours they worked and the difficulty of the cases they reviewed. A curious result occurred.

Although all underwriters performed equally well before the office reassignments began, these office reassignments had a profound effect on productivity.

Those assigned to higher status offices dramatically improved their performance; those assigned to lower status offices dramatically lowered their performance; employees whose workspace rewards were unchanged had performance levels that remained much the same during the study.

As soon as the underwriters returned to their own offices, their performance returned to its original level.

Why did their productivity change? One answer is that people respond to, and correct, inequities created not only by the money they receive, but also other rewards such as the status value of their offices. Therefore if people in a state of equity get more they work harder; take things away, they produce less.

But what is equity?. Consider the example of a group of friends going out for a meal who agree to go Dutch; they usually divide the bill (plus tip) by the number of people present and pay *equally*. Everybody pays the same despite the fact that they have eaten differently priced dishes. This means, of course, that those who choose modestly priced food and drink tap water *subsidise* those who have more expensive tastes and drink alcohol.

As a consequence people who dine together tend to choose dishes of similar cost. They either *all* do or do not have a starter, a drink or dessert so that no one person or group eats more than the others.

If, however, somebody wants an expensive item and the others do not, it is frequently agreed that he or she pays for it separately. The principle of *equality* — people all pay equally irrespective of what they eat is replaced by the principle of *equity* — where people pay differently depending on what they eat.

There is one other option whereby the richest in the group pays proportionally more. This principle, *taxation*, is the least popular.

Nearly everyone faced with the choice argues for equity, certainly in the world of work, and particularly when it comes to pay, nearly everybody favours equity over equality because they feel it is the fairest system. Climate surveys, which are snapshots of a company's health, frequently show people are most unhappy with the pay system because appraisal is not directly linked to pay.

Strikes, walk-outs and go-slows are often the result not of complaints about *absolute* pay but *comparative* pay. Let one person discover that he or she is paid less for work of equal or equivalent skill, responsibility or 'messiness' than a colleague and all hell is let loose.

Where people feel unfairly dealt with and inequitably rewarded — nearly always under-benefited in the sense that they feel they give more than they get — they nearly always attempt to rectify the position. There are two ways working people bring about a sense of pay equity: increase their rewards or decrease their effort (or both).

The first is to get more reward (such as pay) for one's work in terms of money or benefits, sometimes called a package. But that is neither easy nor even feasible in public or poorly performing companies or in a recession.

There are, however, other things people can take. For instance, shoplifting (politely called shrinkage) is more often done by employees than customers, partly because it is easier! Certainly stealing goods is one way of increasing rewards if, of course, one's organization produces or has something worth stealing.

On the other hand, an employee can steal time by coming in late, going early or simply going absent frequently. Time is money and can be relatively easily stolen as national absentee (and especially local council) figures show. The easiest way of achieving equity is to work fewer days for the same money.

It is frequently difficult, dangerous or even impossible to increase rewards; therefore it is much more common to find employees compensating by reducing their input and their enthusiasm for the job, the amount of effort they put into their work, their willingness to do (unpaid) overtime, or their attitudes to the customer.

In the last resort, any worker, convinced that he or she is unfairly dealt with, might leave the organization, therefore the most common reaction is the alienated, uncommitted, unhelpful worker — the sort we have all encountered, even in customer service industries.

Sometimes a feeling of inequity comes after promotion because although promotion usually means an increase in salary, status and benefits, it also means an increase in responsibility and workload and, alas, the two might not increase proportionally.

Some people refuse promotion because although they feel equitably dealt with at their level, on the next level increased responsibilities simply outweigh rewards. Hence the fact that in some jobs people frequently eschew promotion until the equity balance is re-introduced! But most frequently the feeling of inequity and unfairness occurs when we compare ourselves to others doing almost the same job, but in different organizations in different countries.

People at work need to feel fairly and equitably rewarded. Their perception of fairness may differ from their employers because the value attached to rewards (outputs) such as free meals, sports/fitness facilites, company car and inputs (hours of work, attention to detail, customer responses) may not be shared by employer and employee. But if employees feel unfairly dealt with they will generally do something about it.

Not everybody in a state of inequity feels angry because they are underbenefited. Some, so the theory goes, feel guilty because they are over-benefited. To overcome this imbalance, the fortunate inequitably over-benefited can either not take their full benefits or work harder. Margaret Thatcher, the British ex-Prime Minister, did both: she did not take her full Prime Ministerial salary (taking only that of a minister) and worked preposterously long hours. What, one wonders, did she feel guilty about?

> ➤ Maintaining equity in reward systems may be crucial to employee performance.
>
> ➤ When people feel unfairly dealt with and inequitably rewarded, they will generally take steps to try to rectify that position.
>
> ➤ Adverse reactions to inequity tend to have damaging consequences for organizations, performance and productivity.

E. Bottom Up: Getting Subordinates to Assess their Bosses

More and more organizations subscribe to the fundamental ideas of performance management. All employees should be given regular feedback through their carefully monitored and check-list-rated job performance. And these ratings must be related to promotions, merit pay, postings abroad, sideways moves or be used more simply for training purposes. More courageous organizations actually determine pay increments by these ratings so that annual increases and salary are not determined by collective bargaining but rather by rated individual effort. This, of course, means that people in the *same* job, at the *same* level, in the *same* organization are unlikely to receive the same pay, unless quite unusually all perform at the same level. Performance management means true meritocracy. It is also the enemy of most unions which believe rewarding individual merit is the short and slippery slope from equality to equity and a reduction in their role.

In effect, performance management means that once or twice a year a manager is required to fill out a rating form (of varying length, content and complexity) on all those employees reporting to him or her. Depending on the size (big/small) and shape (tall/flat) of the organization, some managers may have to appraise as many as twenty (even fifty) subordinates. This naturally leads to certain problems arising — do the managers know or see all their staff? How much time does it takes to appraise so many? What about problems of favouritism? More importantly, how well do bosses know their employees and their individual work contribution?

Innovative organizations have found simple but radical solutions to these problems. Hence courageous CEOs are changing their old methods. Employees aren't rated by their superiors but by their subordinates. Not top-down but bottom-up. Instead of being rated by the single person you report to, you are rated by *all* those staff who report to you. The appraisal boot, so to speak, is on the other foot. Of course, employees have always judged/rated their boss informally and constantly (mainly through gossip!) but this method attempts to make the implicit explicit.

What are the advantages and dangers in this approach? Simple though it is, and democratic, the idea puts the fear of God into many managers as they have never been rated this way. But, first, what has one to gain via this method?

● Subordinates tend to know their superior more than superiors know their subordinates. They see their bosses and know their moods, foibles and preferences; they know their adequacies, skills, strengths, limitations and things that they do and do not like doing. Anyone who had been managed by a number of bosses knows their idiosyncracies of day-to-day management of tasks, individuals and groups. And being at the sharp end of his/her policies and preferences they are in a privileged position to judge them. Clearly servants know more about their masters than the other way around. Surely, therefore, it is more appropriate that the subordinates rate their bosses, who they know well, rather than that the superiors rate those below them, who they do not know as well.

● Because all subordinates rate their manager from a statistical point of view, these ratings tend to be more reliable — and the more subordinates who supply ratings the better. Instead of the quirks and the biases of individual managers' ratings (some being over-lenient, others strict, some showing favouritism), the various ratings of the employees can be checked for their agreement in the ratings, and then converted so that (hopefully) they can be averaged into a representative, fair view. If the employees have very different views of their bosses (dividing into, say, two quite distinct groups) this can present problems but represent very significant data that merit further investigation. Indeed the patterns in the upward feedback data are very revealing of managers' styles.

● Subordinates' ratings have more impact because it is more unusual to receive ratings by subordinates than by superiors. It is also surprising to bosses because despite frequent protestations to the contrary, information flows down organizations more often, smoothly and comfortably than it flows up. So when it flows up it is quantitatively and qualititatively different. And it is this difference that makes it impactful. But most employees who have been subordinate appraised will tell of their initial anxiety at the prospect, followed by a fair degree of surprise at the result. These may be drawbacks that cannot be ignored. Many cannot anticipate what their staff think or feel which is a bad sign.

What are the dangers of converting the appraisal system to a bottom-up approach?

● Some employees might hold back from giving their frank and fair appraisal of their boss for fear of reprisal. They may also be unused to giving negative feedback or positive feedback for that matter. This can be observed by a 'halo effect' or the over-use of mid-point ratings where neither specific praise nor blame is given, but bland, safe-ratings half-way up the scale are given. But if ratings are anonymous, randomized and from numerous employees, it is doubtful if a boss could detect individuals' ratings and take personal umbrage.

● On the other hand, an anonymous rating might lead some employees to be extremely vindictive to a boss who in the best interests of the company is pushing his/her staff to do better. Individuals who attempt to 'knife' their superior could easily be detected, however, because their ratings would be significantly different from (and much more negative) than their peers. But if the whole subordinate group decides justly or unjustly to give consensually bad feedback they can! Usually, however, consensually negative upward feedback is a sure sign of poor management.

● There are also greater *costs* involved. More forms have to be processed (probably by computer programme) than in the top-down method. Also subordinates need to be given some later training on how (indeed why) to rate individuals without falling into some of the well-known traps. Training courses, paper work and computing software cost money.

Do the benefits outweigh the dangers and disadvantages of the bottom-up system? Certainly the fact that big and innovative companies have persisted with these methods is some indication of the fact that they believe it has noticeable benefits. To some extent initial enthusiasm has been tempered by a healthy scepticism. To put in place the performance management system where bosses are appraised by their staff, the organization needs to trust and value their staff to be honest, fair and constructive. They need also to pay more than lip service to the idea that communication is a two-way process. And more importantly they need to be willing to act on the ratings of subordinates to reward (or not) managers. This takes some courage and for large multinationals, real culture change. In other words, the organizational culture must already exist for such a system to work. As some have found, there is a lot of resistance to such innovation if the culture is not right.

We are hearing a lot these days about the 'upside-down' organization — the idea that for many companies the lowest paid, trained and rewarded have the most impact because it is they who interface with the customer. And customer satisfaction is the key for successful, service-related business. It is the most junior employees who, in the current jargon, experience most 'moments of truth'. And the way that they are managed is reflected in how they treat the customer.

The bottom-up approach is the first step in the process of taking staff opinions seriously and allowing the staff to influence *up* the organization. This is especially important in service organizations (like airlines, hotel chains, etc) where the treatment of customers depends very much on the way staff are treated by their manager. Most of the companies who have tried the bottom-up method remain in favour of it. Going one step further it could be that employees get individually and systematically appraised by a random selection of customers and that their ratings determine pay. But for many that may be going too far. Nethertheless, the management toast for the successful go-ahead service-related business is a good one: not '*Down* the Hatch' but 'Bottom(s) *Up*'!

➤ In most organizations people are appraised by their superiors who may or may not know them very well.

➤ It is possible and healthy, if somewhat unusual, to be rated and given feedback not top-down from superiors, but bottom-up, from subordinates who know and experience the consequences of management style best.

➤ Although there may be some dangers and disadvantages of upward appraisal, many of these can be anticipated and dealt with.

➤ Upward feedback can be used for personal development, training or actual merit appraisal. It is particularly useful for managers who do not elicit the views of their staff.

➤ Upward feedback may help significantly in the two way communication up and down organizations.

4
MANAGEMENT TECHNIQUES

This section concentrates on three issues. The first is often the bane of managerial life -namely attending meetings. It is frequently argued that meetings are highly inefficient, though they need not be.

The second issue concerns the use of surveys in organizations, which have long been a popular way for senior managers to find out what the rank and file feel and think about their organization.

The third concerns the popular but often ineffective method to generate ideas — brainstorming. In fact research has long demonstrated that it is only under very specific circumstances that traditional brainstorming actually works.

"As your Chairman, I was concerned to make this a truly representative meeting"

A. When not to Have Meetings

A meeting is a group of people who keep minutes and waste hours. Yet surveys show that the average middle-to-senior manager may spend as much as 40% of the working day in meetings. The number of committees, sub-committees, task-force groups, and board meetings which business people are required to attend grows exponentially with rank.

Meetings are well known to be inefficient. As a result they are indispensable when one does not actually want to do anything but still give the appearance of working. Meetings can stifle ideas, postpone and prevaricate. A committee meeting is often a cul-de-sac down which ideas are lured to their death. No grand idea has ever emerged from a committee meeting, which has been described as a group of the unwilling, picked from the unfit, to do the unnecessary!

Given the widespread and justifiable scepticism and cynicism about the usefulness of meetings, why are they so popular? They may be seen as a good way to pool resources. Similarly it has been argued that group members may stimulate and encourage each other through their mutual discussions, in what is known as the synergy effect. Others talk about them being an efficient and democratic way to communicate with people. Still others believe that committees make better decisions and come up with qualitatively and quantitatively better solutions to problems.

These reasons are far from water-tight, however, and there is research evidence which leads one to doubt them. Most meetings are held not to make decisions but to avoid them. Further, they are mainly about diffusion of responsibility, so that if a wrong, poor, costly or even litigious decision is made, fault is spread over all the committee members. Committee meetings are about covering your back by not having to take personal responsibility for important decisions.

There are three major problems with meetings that render them inefficient. The first is sometimes called *social loafing* which refers to the fact that people tend to work less hard (loaf) when in (social) groups than when alone. This phenomenon is discussed in more detail on p.132

Thus, the greater the number of persons in the group, the less the impact such force will have upon each other. Because they are working together, each group member feels that the others will take up any slack resulting from reduced effort on his/her own part. And since all members tend to respond in this fashion, average output per person drops sharply.

The second problem is called by psychologists *evaluation apprehension.*

Basically it suggests that when trying to make decisions in groups, the presence of some group members may intimidate others. Furthermore, disagreement and the voicing of unpopular, if correct, ideas may breed conflict and ill will and may be a bad career move.

It should come as no surprise that high status persons in organizations, such as presidents, chief executives and board chairpersons, are carefully listened to, and what they have to say is given high credence. As a result, high status persons tend to dominate group situations, and their ideas (right and wrong) are frequently accepted without question. The result can easily be a group of 'yes men/women' behind the single dominant force. With an understanding of this phenomenon, former General Motors head Alfred P. Sloan failed to attend the early phase of his group's meetings. He feared that his presence would discourage open and honest discussions of critical problems among other executives, who would insist on pleasing him. Sloan can be complimented on his insight into group dynamics. Indeed, there is every reason to believe that his high status would have had an undue impact on the group by inadvertently encouraging uniformity.

The third problem is quite simply that in creative tasks, groups, rather than individuals working alone, produce qualitatively and quantitatively poorer decisions. In contrast to well-structured tasks that can be divided into several discrete parts and have a definite solution, many everyday management decisions are more poorly structured. Any problem involving creative thinking provides a good example. Suppose an organization is faced with deciding what to do about the prospect of a declining market for its products in the coming years. There are many possible courses of action, and you would probably expect that a group meeting together would do a better job of handling such a problem than any one individual. However, this is generally not the case. Most of the research has shown that on poorly structured, problem solving, creative tasks, individuals show superior performance to groups. This generalization has particularly important — and potentially devastating — implications for organizations, since some administrators spend as much as eighty per cent of their time in committee meetings.

As for business meetings then, the fewer the better. The weekly staff or board meeting may be useful for sharing information though not useful for problem solving. But it is best to follow some simple rules:

1 Start on the dot, no matter who is missing.

2 Why not have meetings standing up? The Privy Council wisely adopts this rule.

3 Go around the room to ensure full participation.

4 Every so often have a secret ballot on whether the regular meetings are necessary.

In general, it is only the minority of time wasters who are meeting addicts. By all means pool ideas and evaluate them but don't have a meeting to generate them.

If a camel is a horse designed by a committee, it probably took much longer than necessary and you can be sure that none of the meetings began on time.

➤ On average, a middle-to-senior level manager may spend 40 per cent of his/her working day in meetings.

➤ Despite cynicism about their effectiveness as a management technique, meetings remain a popular pastime in most organizations.

➤ Problems with meetings stem from individuals not contributing fully to them; intimidation of some participants by others who are present; and their inappropriateness in relation to certain types of decision making.

➤ Meetings should be limited in number and duration, conducted in a highly controlled and disciplined fashion with close adherence to a clearly defined agenda.

B. How to Make the Most of Employee Surveys

Employee attitude surveys have become extremely fashionable. Such surveys aim to establish how people in an organization feel about issues such as job satisfaction, pay, career prospects and the working environment. Conducted properly they can provide an organization's management with systematic insights into staff sensitivities and satisfaction, offer guidance to future management policy and assess employees' reactions to any changes which take place to their working conditions. Employee surveys can find out if the vision the leader has about the organization and where it is going has effectively permeated the workforce. Surveys can also help to pinpoint problem areas relating to different aspects of organizational functioning which may underlie low morale or poor performance.

Attitude surveys can be carried out among the whole workforce or they can focus on particular groups or sections whose opinions management are especially interested to measure. Such surveys can be used to audit staff perceptions relating to corporate climate, communications systems and customer service orientations. They can also feature as a component of a culture audit.

Employee attitude surveys are becoming increasingly popular. In the United Kingdom, they are an American import, with the early users being US companies such as Mars, Kodak and IBM.

IBM has conducted regular surveys of its UK employees — half of them one year, the other half the next — on their attitudes to matters such as workplace communications, motivation, trust and their understanding of corporate goals. While companies such as IBM make conscientious attemps to translate findings into action, other organizations may waste considerable sums of money on projects which raise employees' expectations only to be shelved or disregarded.

Attitude surveys can act as a safety valve that allows people to blow off steam instead of harbouring grievances. However, the mere fact that the research is being conducted is an intervention in the working lives of employees which may itself produce shifts in attitudes or more importantly, can raise employees' expectations that the company is listening to them and will implement action plans on the basis of the feedback they provide. Thus, it is vital that organizations do not take the implications of employee attitude surveys lightly. Staff will want to see the results and know how they are going to be used. Far too many companies conduct staff attitude surveys as a reflex action to perceived problems. Many companies become immersed in technical matters such as questionnaire design, without first being clear what the survey is for and what will be done with the results.

Apart from conducting the survey, the most important thing is to act on it. The most effective way to win co-operation and commitment is for at least some of the organization's actions to come in response to employees' feelings and suggestions. Nothing is more counter-productive than to spend a lot of money listening to what they say and then do nothing about it.

Employee surveys rarely come cheap. Indeed, their costs to the organization can be felt in ways other than purely budgetary ones. As well as the direct financial expense of paying for the survey, which can escalate considerably if a big name outside consultancy is used, there are also the organizational costs to be considered. When employees are surveyed they are likely to ask why. The survey may be perceived as a management mechanism for checking up on them. Even if they accept that the organization means well, however, they will not only expect to be told the results but also to see how their employer intends to act upon the findings. Sometimes, the action steps may turn out to be ones with which management does not feel comfortable.

Given the potential costs, it is essential that organizations which undertake employee surveys obtain the maximum value from them. All too often, however, this doesn't happen. Simplistic, standard forms of data analysis and interpretation mean that the information of significance from the survey is not laid before management.

The typical survey report presents a description of surface attitudes within the organization. The company is told what proportion of its employees in general, or within specific departments and sections, agree with particular opinions or points of view. Displayed in simple percentage terms and in charts, such results provide a visible profile of employee perceptions of different aspects of organizational functioning.

What this sort of report does not tell the company is *why* its employees hold particular attitudes. It does not provide any indication of relationships between different attitudes. For instance, do individuals who hold a favourable view about one part of the organization respond similarly towards some other part of it? Nor is there usually any attempt to explore the predictive capability of the data. Are perceptions of specific parts of the organization or terms of employment more significant than others to general job satisfaction, employee morale or job performance?

A case example serves to illustrate this point. One international company in the finance sector surveyed its employees around the world to investigate their perception of and attitudes towards various forms of corporate communication. These included corporate videos, magazines and newsletters, notices and meetings. Other general attitudes about organizational management style and communications were also measured (including four items which broadly referred to morale-type views). The company's consultants reported back on the claimed frequency with which employees received or experienced each type of communication, on attitudes towards specific communications and on general corporate communications attitudes. These results were apparently found to be informative by the company, which reported back to employees in staff magazines and newsletters.

What the report did not reveal, however, was whether employees who claimed that they often received one form of communication also received any of the others. It did not indicate whether employees with higher frequencies of reception of particular types of communication also held them in higher or lower esteem. Nor was there any attempt to find out if employees who more often received many different kinds of company communications tended to have higher morale, even though the data were available.

A recent research programme launched by the authors at the Business Psychology Unit, University College London, has begun to explore ways in which organizations can make more effective use of their employee survey data. In a study which has applied special statistical techniques which can measure degrees of association and predictive relationships between survey variables, organizations are shown how to extract more valuable corporate information from employee research.

With one participating company, in the private sector, a range of techniques was applied to climate survey findings to reveal that employees' attitudes about the organization were not to be conceived purely in terms of the questionnaire category headings, as is so often the case in employee attitude survey reports. Correlational and factor analysis techniques revealed that, at a superordinate level, staff perceptions of their employer took on a different psychological profile from those assumed by management on their behalf.

Another technique, multiple regression analysis, was able to identify groups of attitudes and biographical details of employees (e.g., gender, age, grade, length of service, etc) which significantly predicted their general job satisfaction and level of pride in their organization. In this specific case, perceptions that good work is recognised and rewarded, together with the degree of variety in their job, emerged as the two significant predictors of job satisfaction. Enjoyment of working for the organization, job variety, clarity of job description, and belief that the organization knows what it is doing emerged as significant predictors of pride in their employer.

What these results provide is an indication to management of which aspects of the organization or of employees' working conditions they should address if they wish to effect specific changes to job satisfaction or pride in the company. Of course, a company may not be interested in these two phenomena. The same techniques can be applied, however, to any other target variables which the organization's management is concerned about. If the required data have been obtained in the survey, management have at their disposal a potentially valuable information source to guide future policy or change decisions — and one that is based on feedback from employees themselves.

If an organization has taken the often difficult decision to conduct a survey among its employees, it should try to obtain the maximum benefit possible from it. Typical descriptive reports showing simple attitude profiles only scratch the surface. Beneath this visible surface it is possible to find latent information which reveals far more about the organization. The right statistical key can unlock a goldmine of knowledge which enables employee survey findings to be applied more widely and with greater effect.

> ➤ Many organizations carry out employee attitude surveys. These surveys can supply valuable insights into the climate of opinion about the way the organization is run among employees at different levels.
>
> ➤ Although increasingly popular, many organizations fail to get full value from these surveys.
>
> ➤ Recent studies have demonstrated ways in which employee surveys can be analysed to yield explanations of staff problems and predictive indicators of desired outcomes.
>
> ➤ Organizations embarking on staff surveys need to give more careful thought to ways of maximizing the informational value of such exercises.

C. Does Brainstorming Work?

Can creativity be taught? How do we come up with a really innovative idea? What is the best method for generating ideas? For many, the answer to these problems is brainstorming. The dictionary definition of a brain-storm is, curiously, 'temporary mental upset marked by uncontrolled emotion and violent action'. But does it work as a creative technique?

Brainstorming is used most frequently to generate as many solutions to a particular problem as possible and thus quantity is favoured over quality. The product of a brainstorming session is ideally a wide range of possible conclusions (options, solutions) which can be presented to a third party qualified to pick the best one. The basic assumption is that 'two heads are better than one' and that together, in groups, innovative solutions can be found. But does brainstorming work? It can, but only under very special circumstances, and indeed it may have in it the seeds of its own destruction.

The technique or rules of brainstorming are quite simple. The first is free-wheeling. Participants are encouraged to be different, to break the mould, to be over-inclusive and allow any crazy idea or association into the solution. Self-censorship is discouraged and nothing is unacceptable.

The second rule is no *criticism*. In order to encourage the near-psychotic activity of wild ideas association, the participants should not be put off by the disapproval of others. Neither the sotto voce hiss nor the raised eyebrow is tolerated because these are off-putting to idea producers. At this stage all ideas, however way out, (indeed because they are unusual) are equally valuable.

The third rule is that piggy-backing is OK. This means that it is quite acceptable to jump on the back of others; to run with their ideas and to follow someone down an unusual path. Indeed this is precisely why this activity is group-oriented. Groups supposedly give one synergy and energy, and provide stimulation. But do they? In all circumstances? The evidence suggests that group-working might not be the best stimulus to creativity in all conditions. An important determinant of whether decisions are better made by groups or by individuals rests in one of the characteristics of the problem: how well structured or poorly structured is the issue about which a decision is to be made?

Imagine working on a problem that requires several very specific steps and has a definite right or wrong answer, such as an arithmetic problem or an anagram puzzle. How can one expect to perform on such a well structured task when working alone compared to when working with a group of people? Research findings indicate that groups performing well structured tasks tend to make better, more accurate decisions, but take more time to reach them than individuals. In one study, subjects worked either individually or in groups of five on several well structured problems. Comparisons between groups and individuals were made with respect to accuracy (the number of problems solved correctly) and speed (the time it took to solve the problems). It was found that the average accuracy of groups of five persons working together was greater than the average accuracy of five individuals working alone. However, it was also found that groups were substantially slower (by as much as 40%) than individuals in reaching solutions.

It is interesting to consider the reasons why these and other similar results arise. The potential advantage that groups might enjoy is being able to pool their resources and combine their knowledge to generate a wide variety of approaches to problems. For these benefits to be realized, however, it is essential that the group members have the necessary knowledge and skills to contribute to the group's task. In short, for there to be a beneficial effect of pooling of resources, there has to be something to pool. Two heads may be better than one only when neither is a blockhead; the 'pooling of ignorance' does not help at all.

But most of the problems faced by organizations are *not* well structured. They do not have any obvious steps or parts, and there is no obviously right or wrong answer. Such problems are referred to as poorly structured. Creative thinking is required to make decisions on poorly structured tasks. For example, a company deciding how to use a newly developed chemical in its consumer products is facing a poorly structured task. Other poorly structured tasks include: coming up with a new product name, image or logo; or finding new or original uses for familiar objects like a coat-hanger, paper clip or brick. Although one might expect that the complexity of such creative problems would give groups a natural advantage, this is not the case. In fact, research has shown that on poorly structured, creative tasks, individuals perform better than groups. Specifically, in one study people were given 35 minutes to consider the consequences of everybody suddenly going blind. Comparisons were made of the number of ideas/issues/outcomes generated by groups of four or seven people and a like number of individuals working on the same problem alone. Individuals were far more productive than groups and arrived at their answers much faster.

The relative ineffectiveness of brainstorming groups has also been demonstrated in a recent study where practising managers and management graduate students worked on a fictitious moon survival problem. Participants were asked to imagine that they have crash-landed on the moon 200 miles from their base. They then ranked, in order of importance to their survival, the pieces of equipment they had intact. It was found that the quality of decisions made by interacting groups was no better than that of the best individual group member. In another study using this same problem, the investigators found that it is essential for the contributions of the most qualified group members to be counted most heavily in the group's decisions, in order for the group to derive the benefits of that member's presence. Thus, in some groups the people who gave the best, most correct answers were ignored by the group members whose greater insistence but poorer ideas carried the day.

Thus what the research seems to indicate is highly counter-intuitive to many. Most brainstorming is used by creative organizations which care little about the skill composition of the problem-solving groups who are then confronted with poorly structured tasks such as thinking of the name for a new product. In other words, brainstorming is used when it is least effective, and rarely when it is most effective.

How does brainstorming translate into other languages? For a non-native speaker it may be associated linguistically with an epileptic fit or a splitting headache. Certainly, for some people the experience of taking part in this activity to solve a creative, open-ended task leads to a migraine. The paradox of brainstorming is that this technique is most frequently used when research suggests it is least effective.

➤ Brainstorming is group problem-solving with special rules to encourage creativity.

➤ It has been conclusively demonstrated that brainstorming produces better solutions, rather slower than if done individually, but only to structured, logical, 'correct answer' problems.

➤ Brainstorming is frequently used where it has been shown individuals working alone produce qualitatively and quantitatively better answers.

➤ 'Group-think', or the power of social groups to influence individuals is largely responsible for brainstorming frequently failing.

➤ With able people and a structured problem, choose group brain-storming; under all other conditions pool solutions that are individually thought-through.

D. Getting Ideas from Employees

Increasing numbers of organizations are trying out schemes in which staff are given opportunities to offer their ideas about work systems and practices. Comments may be invited orally or in writing. Such employee participation programmes (EPPs) as quality circles and staff suggestion schemes have become especially popular. The purpose of these programmes is to make employees feel that their opinion counts and that they can play an active part in determining how the organization is run. At the same time, some of the ideas generated may result in improved work procedures of benefit to the organization and everyone in it.

Employee participation schemes have not been universally accepted as producing real benefits, however. There is evidence that EPPs can enhance employees' attitude toward work. Whether or not such schemes lead to improved performance is less clear. How positively employees respond to EPPs, however, can depend upon a number of factors.

One important variable is how actively employees normally participate in policy-related decisions in their own organization. Some people want to have a say in how things are run at work. They show what has been called 'organizational citizenship behaviour'. Another factor is the degree of unhappiness over opportunities to be involved in important decisions which affect their work situations.

There are various techniques organizations can use to solicit employees' comments and ideas. Very often employees' good ideas about how to improve work procedures and systems fail to have an impact because the individuals who have these ideas don't know how to reach the people with the authority to implement them.

Suggestion boxes offer one way of getting around this problem. Employees are invited to write their ideas down and place them in boxes which are emptied every week. The cards are read by the chief executive and other senior managers who decide which ones to take action on. Research has found that about fifteen per cent of employees use their companies' suggestion boxes and that about twenty-five per cent of the suggestions made are implemented.

Once regarded as only being appropriate in large manufacturing companies, suggestion schemes have increasingly found favour in white collar organizations like banks and buildings societies. And while large organizations such as British Airways and the Inland Revenue run successful schemes, some privately owned businesses and small divisions in large companies have also found them to be of considerable value.

At the beginning of the 1990s the Industrial Society estimated that there were between 400 and 500 staff suggestion schemes in operation in Britain. The UK Association of Suggestion Schemes (UKASS), founded in 1987, has over 100 members.

A survey by the Industrial Society in 1988 showed that the 103 schemes identified had received more than 73,400 suggestions or five for every 100 employees. Just over 16,000 suggestions were adopted, a success rate of 22 per cent.

The traditional view of suggestion schemes was that they were a way of saving a company money. Since employees were so closely involved in the details of manufacturing a particular product they were well placed to suggest ways of making it more quickly or cheaply.

Employees are usually rewarded for their successful suggestions either with a flat monetary bonus or some percentage of the money saved by implementing the scheme.

The oldest continuously operating suggestion system has been in operation at the Eastman Kodak Company since 1898. Since then over two million suggestions have been made at Kodak. The biggest reward of nearly $48,000 was made to an employee who suggested mounting film boxes on cards for display racks at retail stores.

Dunlop General Rubber Products, a Manchester-based subsidiary of the BTR group, reduced waste and saved £7,500 a year when it took up an employee's suggestion to change the way it cut the foam rubber used in vehicle mats.

This was just one of between 150 and 200 suggestions made each year by the 210 employees eligible for the scheme (about 35 managers and senior staff may not participate). Dunlop rewards suggestions which are adopted with a cash payment of 20 per cent of the value of the annual saving up to a maximum of £1,000.

While many suggestions do enable companies to save money, schemes are being increasingly used to make improvements in areas such as quality or customer care where savings, if any, are difficult to quantify.

In addition, many companies believe suggestion schemes can make a contribution to staff morale, showing people that their contribution to the company is valued.

In order to succeed, suggestion schemes must meet a number of criteria.

● They must be carefully planned and provided with the resources and management backing to sustain them over the long term.

● They require constant promotion within the organization lest employees forget about an ongoing scheme or feel it has been discontinued when in fact it hasn't.

● Suggestion schemes should be fun. Some companies give away pens, mugs or badges to suggesters. Special short-term suggestion schemes which focus on particular topics can also enliven proceedings and generate renewed enthusiasm and participation.

● Suggestions must be handled quickly and efficiently. If employees get excited about the outcome of a suggestion they have put forward, they should not be kept waiting more than twenty-four hours before hearing the outcome.

● If suggestions are turned down, employees should be encouraged to submit new ones and not to become discouraged if their most recent attempts fail.

● Suggestions should be rewarded, though opinions differ on the scale of payment. Rewards should be significant, though not too frequent. The Industrial Society has noted, from schemes it surveyed, that rewards paid out amount to around 18 per cent of the savings made.

Another method of providing important information is through corporate hotlines, telephone lines staffed by corporate personnel ready to answer employees' questions, or listen to their comments and suggestions. One example of this kind of staff communication scheme is the 'Let's Talk' programme that AT & T developed in the United States to answer its employees' questions at the time of the company's antitrust divestiture. By providing staff with easy access to information, companies benefit in several ways. It not only shows employees that the company cares for them, but also encourages them to address their concerns before the issues become more serious. In addition, by keeping track of the kinds of questions and concerns voiced, top management is given a good source of feedback about the things that are on employees' minds. Such information can be invaluable when attempting to improve conditions within the organization.

A further approach to involving and obtaining information from employees is quality circles. These consist of small groups of volunteers, usually around ten, who meet regularly, typically on a weekly basis, to identify and solve problems related to their jobs and work conditions. An organization might have several quality circles operating at once, each dealing with a particular area about which it has the most expertise. Some kind of training is generally advised for circle members to enable them to become effective problem solvers. The outcomes and recommendations of quality circles are fed upwards to senior management.

Research has shown that while quality circles are very effective at producing short-term improvements in aspects of work quality, they are less effective at creating permanent changes. As such they may be regarded as useful in respect of temporary changes to enhance effectiveness at work.

There are a variety of benefits (even if short-term ones) that might result from quality circle and other employee feedback schemes. One direct benefit is increased job satisfaction and commitment of employees to the organization. Increased productivity may also be achieved. Following on from these benefits is a third positive outcome — increased organizational effectiveness. Many large companies such as Ford, General Electric, and AT & T have been pleased with the results of active employee participation programmes.

Benefits do not follow automatically. EPP success depends on the full cooperation of management and staff at the design and implementation stages. Plans agreed to by all parties must then be fully implemented. It is too easy to allow certain action plans to be forgotten amongst all the other work activities that fill each day. Responsibility for an EPP must be assumed by employees of all levels to follow through on their part of the programme.

➤ Organizations are using employee participation programmes as a way of generating new business ideas and to enhance employee commitment to the organizaiton.

➤ Various techniques have been tried involving suggestion boxes, quality circles and corporate hotlines.

➤ The success of these programmes depend critically upon careful planning, regular promotion, making them interesting to participants and appropriate scales of research for suggestions taken up.

➤ Corporate benefits will best avoid difficulty if staff and management cooporate fully during design and implementation stages of employee participation programmes.

E. Benchmarking

Most of us can remember, in response to the concerned parent or considerate friend who asks 'How did you get on?' in some test or exam, replying with confidence, '78 per cent'. But what we concealed was that we were in fact bottom of the class.

Although business performance can be measured objectively and as an absolute in any free enterprise situation, it is crucial to take into consideration the competition. Market share is, of course, a well-known business performance indicator. Organizations are now encouraged more and more to do extensive 'benchmarking' of their products, procedures and processes.

In an increasingly competitive and sophisticated business world, however, organizations are finding that reliance on one index of comparison with others is not enough. As such, more and more companies are turning to 'benchmarking' in order to gauge their own performance relative to others on a whole range of business procedures and practices. Benchmarking represents continuous improvement of what an organization does by learning how other organizations do it.

Benchmarking, as a management technique, came into prominence during the 1980s. It is designed to supply management with practices that deliver customer value. Companies have found that it is an extremely helpful tool enabling them to find out where they are in terms of practice.

The benefits of benchmarking are quite simply that all organizational functions are forced to investigate external industry best practices and compare these to their own operations.

By making benchmarking a line management responsibility, managers are encouraged to probe the underlying business procedures and practices that characterize their own organization's treatment of its customers.

The power of benchmarking was underlined in the case of Xerox, where it is indicated as being one of the main factors behind the company's revival in the 1980s. Xerox embarked on competitive benchmarking with its Japanese subsidiary Fuji Xerox in the early 1980s. One of the main findings of the analysis of Japanese competitors was that Canon could sell a photocopier for less than it cost Xerox in the USA to manufacture one. Since then Xerox has moved from studying competitors to evaluating companies in industries as varied as railways, insurance and electricity generators. This has enabled the company to identify best practice ways of improving aspects of its business ranging from timeliness to customer satisfaction and retention, and statistical process control.

There are a number of features central to benchmarking. first, it must be a continuous process because the competition constantly changes. Secondly, it aims at certain specific objective metrics of comparison. Thirdly, it can and should apply to all facets of the business' products, services and practices. And finally, perhaps most importantly, benchmarking should not be aimed solely at direct product competitors, but those recognized as industry leaders.

But, whether dignified with the handle 'benchmarking' or simply called competitor comparisons, the process has obvious benefits. It enables the best practices from any industry to be creatively incorporated into the practices of the benchmarked function. It can provide ideas and motivation to those who have to implement the benchmarked findings.

Benchmarking may break down much ingrained reluctance to certain operations. People seem more receptive to new ideas and their adoption when the ideas do not originate in their own industry, perhaps because they are already tried and tested, and have proved successful. Conversely, the 'not invented here' syndrome can undermine the benchmarking process. Many managers believe their own corporate circumstances to be unique, special and unlikely to respond to competitors' innovations.

Benchmarking may also identify technological breakthroughs and determine cost-benefits that may be achieved if they are, or are not, incorporated in its own operations. There are also 'networking' benefits for the benchmarkers who may broaden their professional contacts and interactions.

In theory benchmarking is not simply a mechanism for determining resources reduction. It is not a panacea or a programme — it is an ongoing process with a structured methodology. It is not a cookbook, though certain steps can be followed. It aims to focus on the competition and to compare internal actions against the external standards of the industry. It can promote cohesion and teamwork by directing attention towards business practices to remain competitive rather than personal individual interest.

Competitor performance can be charted through customer surveys which examine customers' perceptions of a company's own performance compared with that of its competitors in a general sense, or with regard to specific aspects of products or services supplied.

Benchmarking is an ongoing comparison process that attempts to ensure that best industry practices are uncovered, analyzed, adopted and implemented. The Japanese, master mimics and copiers, are well known for it. So why don't all companies do it routinely?

Benchmarking may not be appropriate for every company. It may be best suited to organizations which have embraced corporate change or renewal programmes, such as total quality management. Competitor audits, however, can usefully be carried out in most types of service organization. A company should itself try out the products and services of its major competitors and survey customers for their opinions about competitors. A company can benchmark aspects of its own performance by comparing itself with competitors on common performance criteria. This type of audit can help a company identify where it is placed in the quality league within its market sector.

Like all business ideas, benchmarking is sold by some consultants and business writers as an essential element in business success. Of course it has limitations. Focusing on competitor's performance can, if undisciplined, simply divert attention from the ultimate purpose of the process. Benchmarking solely against competitors may also uncover practices that are not optimal or worthy of evaluation and hence a waste of effort. Furthermore, competitive benchmarking may lead to meeting the competitors' position, but it will not necessarily lead to creating practices superior to those of the competition.

Just as some organizations resist doing staff surveys because they don't want to know what the state of morale is in their organization, so they resist the process of benchmarking for fear it will highlight their own shortcomings. Others arrogantly believe they are already aware of the fundamental differences between their own and their competitors' operations and don't need to waste time and money on the process.

➤ More and more organizations are turning to benchmarking to compare their own business practices and performance with those of competitors.

➤ The essence of benchmarking is to learn how to operate more productively and profitably by studying the best business procedure practised elsewhere.

➤ Benchmarking, to be effective, needs to be carried out as a regular process because competition is continually changing. It needs to cover all major facets of a business.

➤ In order to combine real business benefits, a benchmarking exercise must compare with a good sample of competitors. When best industry practices are uncovered an organization must have the ability to integrate such priorities within its own operations.

➤ Merely evaluating competitors may lead to performance which equals, but does not exceed, theirs. Learning from benchmarking needs to lead to a creation of even better business practices than those employed by the competitors.

5

PROBLEMS OF MANAGEMENT

Management is not easy and takes intelligence and skill. Indeed that is one reason why managers are better paid than employees.

This section deals, amongst other things, with how and why some fail at management. It also looks at the problems of making scientists and technical wizards into managers.

A second theme is about communication within organizations and the confusion of the message with the medium.

Managers succeed and fail for different reasons. Having a simple category scheme helps senior managers to diagnose problems and therefore to treat them correctly. Also understanding the problems of promoting specialists into management jobs can be helpful.

"To say that promoting Dr. Collins is creating a monster is a bit strong Gerald…"

A. Diagnosing Management Failure

Every organization has its dead wood. Some managers are promoted to their own level of incompetency. Others are chronic underachievers (people with fine futures behind them!) bewildered by the twentieth century. Still others are the lame ducks of bureaucratic systems, keeping their heads down and doing anything for a quiet life.

Management failures are inefficient — but worse they are embarrassing, expensive and set a bad example to younger staff who (as yet) have not fallen into bad ways. Because prevention is better than cure, one way organizations can deal with a problem is through judicious recruitment and selection, to weed out potential or actual management failures. It is not easy 'letting people go' if they don't want it, and it is not good for the ego to admit a selection failure. But it happens in all organizations. There are people at all levels who are incompetent and inefficient. Why?

Managers fail for a variety of reasons, but essentially these can be categorized into six general causes.

Capacity: Some managers simply don't have the ability to do the job. Some people are naturals with numbers, others with words; some are highly intuitive and creative while others are skilful at solving logical problems. Scientific boffins have difficulty managing people, while good man-managers may sometimes have difficulty understanding graphic displays and formulaes. Replicated studies have shown that in some jobs (particularly selling) there is a negative correlation between intelligence and job success. This is particularly true of salesmen and if they are promoted into strategic management roles they probably will not be able to cope. There is quite simply a limit to the ability or capacity that people have in certain areas. Capacity is a kinder word than either intelligence or ability but has similar implications. Some managers fail because, quite simply, they don't have the intellectual horse power required for the job. And there is a limit to which people can be trained if they do not have any natural ability.

Learning: Major and significant changes at work, particularly in information technology but also in management practices, has meant that some managers have been left behind. They bumble, stumble and mumble because they have not been taught 'the new ways'. The mysteries of the word processor, the appraisal scheme and fax machine need to be explained. The solution is, of course, to send them on an in-house or outside training course that is relevant, practical and suitable to their needs and abilities. Companies need to ensure that these do not appear to employees as jolly junkets or entertaining free lunches, but rather as necessary and salient for their future development and promotability. But, self-evidently, not all training courses work: they must be carefully designed for the needs of the individual and the skills being taught!

Motivation: The same job can appear to different individuals as tediously boring, interesting and captivating, or painfully stressful. Extraverts prefer jobs with variety, social contact and sensory stimulation, while introverts prefer a more stable, predictable work environment, often of the 'man-machine' rather than 'person to person' variety. Most managers select jobs that fit their personality though not all are successful. Others are promoted to different sorts of jobs that do not suit them and boredom or stress can arise. It is alas a truism, but also true, that square pegs in round holes are demotivated. A number of solutions are possible for this problem: career counselling; job enrichment; a sideways move; the introduction of various controls — all aimed at getting optimal performance and motivation from a manager. Poor motivation is one of the most common problems at work but frequently misunderstood.

Distraction: Inevitably a manager's private life affects his or her job. Marital problems, children, economic and health factors in the family can each have a powerful effect on a manager's well being. Just as a stable, happy family life can promote adjustment and allow a manager to cope with added work stress so family problems of all sorts can not only increase stress but break an otherwise robust manager's coping mechanisms. A failing manager may be distracted by personal issues outside the work place such that he or she can not concentrate in their working world. This is a tricky problem for organizations, which may involve them sponsoring some form of counselling. Indeed, one of the traditional roles of the personnel department is to help employees over distracting personal problems.

Alienation: If managers themselves have been managed very badly for a long period of time they may become quite indifferent to either carrots or sticks. The alienated manager may be corrupt, capricious and irascible and is nearly always inefficient. Large state-run industries and bureaucracies have their fair share of these individuals who, protected from customers, clients and market forces, can happily underachieve for years. These cases are difficult to cure and managers of newly privatized companies are finding out. Most employees need a short sharp shock every once in a while to see the relationship between effort and reward.

Personality: It is true that there is a systematic relationship between personality and managerial incompetence. Certain types — the likeable chameleon, the vengeful psychopath and the nascent narcissist — can be dangerously incompetent precisely because they are difficult to spot. It is debatable how easy personality is to change so it is not always easy to know what to advise employers if their employee's personality is perceived to be the cause of a problem. Personality as a catch-all explanation is far too frequently offered by people in business. It is, however, an unlikely cause of incompetence.

Diagnosis precedes cure and treatment. Not only is the treatment costly and pointless — it might even be dangerous if incorrectly applied. Sending a person on a training course for a capacity problem is a waste of money, and job enrichment for the distracted is pointless. Human resource and personnel managers need to be able to diagnose the major cause why managers in their organization fail and hence offer workable solutions. The real underlying reason for incompetence and inefficiency is essentially sixfold and requires a suitable response for each. Understanding why managers fail is the first step to ensuring corporate excellence.

➤ If someone is accused of being inefficient or incompetent check that the evidence for the accusation is valid and reliable.

➤ Consider the causes of this problem: use the six diagnosis points as a check-list in one or more of these problems.

➤ Make the cure follow from the diagnosis. Ensure that the solution follows from the problem and therefore can solve it.

➤ Remember that frequent changes in organizational structure, everyday technology, management style and personal circumstances can easily render the competent manager incompetent and vice-versa!

B. The Technical Boffin as Manager

It is an almost universal truth that the more one gets promoted in a job the less one actually exercises the skills one initially needed to perform it. Bishops don't convert, professors don't research, generals don't fight: they all manage others who do it.

The same is true in organizations. The financial director doesn't work out profit and loss accounts; the marketing director does not go to brainstorming sessions; and the engineering director is hardly likely to get his hands dirty. Their job is to make sure that others perform the task: that is, to manage. As everyone knows, promotion means more management, administration and delegation responsibilities, and fewer 'hands on' duties.

To some, the skills of management come easily. Understanding, challenging, and supporting staff is easy for 'people-people'. But what of the problems of the introverted, technical specialist, uncomfortable with the 'soft' intuitive skills of general management? What of those introverted, intolerant-of-ambiguity specialists who know a lot about a little... and little else?

There are essentially two responses to the dilemma of promoting the technical expert to a manager. The less preferred and still quite rare response is in fact not to do so. Some organizations agree that boffins are most comfortable, and ultimately most cost-effective, using their technical skills. To train them to be managers is not to 'release' them to do other work, but rather to 'imprison' them in a job they hate, even despise. So, to cope with the problem of promotion for effort, some organizations have a two-track policy. In this binary world, boffins can grow ever more senior but still are not strictly managers. They do what they are good at, what they like doing, and what the organization first lured them for, but at even more senior levels of pay and job title. But in the usual sense of the word they are not managers, though paradoxically they may have the term in their titles.

But most organizations believe that even the most unpromising intellectual, the socially unskilled scientist, or inadequate technician can be turned into a competent manager of others.

People who may get promotion usually have to meet a number of criteria:

● *They need the desire to be a manager.* They must believe that managing people is interesting, stimulating and more importantly, a skill. Hence they must believe and understand that they need to invest considerable time and effort in acquiring these skills, which like all skills need to be learnt, practised and polished.

113

- *They need to have a minimal level of communication skills.* They must feel at ease communicating with people in all branches of the organization, at any level. They must learn how to negotiate, influence, liaise and simply make friends. An introvert can be socialized into looking like a comfortable extravert, though the role may be exhausting for them. Social skills can be taught though they are self-evidently more easily acquired by some rather than others.

- *They must be able to develop an overview of the whole business.* That is, they must understand technological trends, product applications, markets and the economic conditions of the business unit. More importantly, perhaps, they need to be able to communicate with technical colleagues from other disciplines and work as part of a management team. This 'helicopter-view', as some gurus have entitled it, means learning another's priorities and language.

- *They need to be administratively competent.* Every manager must be familiar with basic skills such as planning, scheduling, budgeting, organizing, and negotiating resources. Some of these skills come easily because they are clearly part of the current job, but many patently are not and have to be learnt.

- Most importantly, *managers must have business acumen.* That is, good managers need to feel comfortable working in dynamic environments associated with uncertainty and change. They must be good at directing the activities of their departments toward the overall business objectives of the company. They need to take an interest in and be more knowledgeable about the business as a whole. *The Economist, The Wall Street Journal* and the *financial Times* have to replace the 'Enthusiasts Monthly'.

Personal desire alone is clearly not enough to be good manager. Promotable individuals need to be competent in their current assignments, not people promoted from a position of incompetence. They must also have the capacity to take on greater responsibility. Of course, they have to be prepared for new and very different assignments requiring the acquisition and exercise of new skills. There also needs to be a good fit between the manager's ambitions, desires, and capabilities and the current (and long range) needs of the organization. finally, perhaps most importantly, they need the aptitude for management.

Can these various facets be trained? Most people would agree that some can be relatively easily acquired, especially certain aspects of business knowledge. five-week business courses on marketing, accounting and economics can do wonders for the bright scientist. But can good administrative habits be acquired? With an efficient and sensitive PA, who might be the power behind the throne, the answer is yes. But what about temperament? Can the nervous introvert, more at home with books, computers and technology, be turned into the gregarious extravert now required to manage petulant and capricious workers? The answer is yes, but only with difficulty and cost! A good analogy is speaking a foreign language: one can learn to become pretty fluent but one still has an accent and it is tiring to practise because of the concentration needed.

Like everything else, learning to become a good manager takes effort and ability, and perhaps most of all, the energy, tenacity, and fortitude to acquire the skills. But as all psychotherapists say, only those who really want to change get better.

➤ Promotion as a manager usually means less hands-on exercise of well-trained professional skills, and the acquisition of new skills.

➤ The creative, solitary, boffin has few natural inclinations to management roles and positions.

➤ Should the organization and the boffin desire it, the skills can be taught and a satisfactory level of functioning achieved.

➤ Boffins need to divert, in part, their intelligent inquisitiveness into the issues, problems and constraints of the business and financial world.

➤ For some the change is relatively smooth and ultimately satisfying while for others it is never really satisfactorily accomplished.

C. The Medium for the Message

Some people prefer to communicate certain messages in writing and others using speech. Research has shown that the choice of a communication medium can greatly affect the degree of clarity or ambiguity of the message being sent.

Oral media (eg., telephone conversations and face-to-face meetings) are preferable to written media (eg., notes and memos) when messages are ambiguous (requiring a great deal of assistance in interpreting them), whereas written media are preferable when messages are clear.

Research has shown the more ambiguous the message, the more managers prefer using oral media. The clearer the message, the more managers prefer using written media.

Managers can be sensitive to the degree of effectiveness of different communications media in relation to the type of message they need to send. Not all managers make these kinds of media choices, however. Some managers have been observed to select media at random.

The sensitivity of managers to communications media is related to their own performance at work. Media-sensitive managers have been found to score higher performance ratings than media-insensitive managers. The skill of selecting the appropriate communications medium is an important aspect of a manager's success.

What leads someone to choose one mode or medium of communication rather than another? Why drop a note in a pigeon-hole as opposed to phoning? Why race up three floors only to find the person not in when you could have used an internal phone?

Many people work in buildings of storey upon storey of identical offices, all desperately personalised by posters and pot plants by the inhabitants to reflect their particular uniqueness. Many still have two phones (internal and external, appropriately black and grey in colour) and pigeon-holes for post which can arrive up to three times a day. And every day people get letters, memos and notes, the telephone rings (frequently simultaneously); and colleagues, call in to visit.

One obvious answer to the question of choice of medium is economy and efficiency telephones are faster, letters and memos can be duplicated and so on. However, there are various important psychological advantages and disadvantages to the various media that are well understood but seldom explicitly discussed.

Consider the *letter*. It has a number of obvious advantages. Unlike the telephone call or face-to-face meeting (unless audio or video taped) the letter is a *record* of communication. Hence, it is the preferred medium of lawyers, bureaucrats and others concerned with the extraction of money or information. The letter, particularly if produced on ubiquitous word-processors, may also be *revised*, considered, or altered so that the precise tone, meaning or ambiguity may be communicated (as well as the paragraphs rearranged and the margins justified). Letters are a more *private* means of communication than the telephone or face-to-face meeting and in some instances *cheaper* than other methods.

Curiously, however, two of the major drawbacks of the letter are also the major advantages of this medium. Letters take time and *feedback* is postponed. It is for this reason that bad news and cheques are sent by post. 'Your cheque is in the post' is a famous lie because the time delay may be blamed on a mysterious other (such as the Post Office). People sending cheques, therefore, use the letter so that they can hold on to the money they owe until the very last moment. Some organizations regularly send out cheques with the incorrect date, or in amounts in figures and words that do not match so that they have to be sent back (also in the long-suffering post) thus yielding a further three to six weeks' interest before the money owed is transferred from their account.

We tend to impart bad news in writing when we feel inadequate about dealing with the feedback we might receive. Angry but unassertive people of all ages frequently write *letters* of complaint after receiving poor service, rather than dealing with the matter immediately, often because they are afraid of the negative (or aggressive) feedback that they are likely to receive. Most discover that, just as in the training of a dog, one should 'push their nose into it' directly it has taken place, not at some later point. Possibly the writers of the letters to newspapers are of this kind — interpersonally passive but once seated at the dining room table behind the battered typewriter a demon, assertive and even aggressive, politician is released.

We also write when the feedback is likely to embarrass us. People who have recently become bereaved, and sometimes the dying themselves, often explain how they got many letters, gifts and flowers but strangely people infrequently visit. Curiously they become isolated when they most need the help, support and companionship of others. People don't visit, not because they do not feel compassion, but rather because they feel inadequate, embarrassed and helpless when the bereaved or dying person becomes emotional, talks about (or even asks questions about) the after-life and occasionally expresses anger at those living. It is much easier just to pop down to a local shop and pick up a suitably sombre or inspiring card (shafts of light; bell, book and candle; stained glass window) with well-chosen (glib, bland) words. As people frequently respond in the same medium through which they were initially contacted, the caring friend can expect nothing more threatening than a grateful acknowledgement letter.

Yet another advantage of the letter is the opportunity it offers for impression-management. first there are the letter-heading and logo features as well as the quality of paper. Some people immediately rub the letter heading like a Braille reader just to check it is embossed. Thereafter he or she checks the paper's watermark and can tell you in moments the cost of 100 or 1,000 sheets of the stuff. Business letter-headed notepaper is used to identify with the organization. Letters also allow one to state formally one's qualifications and job title. It would be arrogant, pompous and highly inappropriate to introduce oneself as John Jones M.A., PhD. though in a letter it is quite acceptable, almost desirable and sometimes necessary. Some people even use their signature to attempt to create an impression. Favourable characteristics include size (bigger the better), legibility (totally illegible if possible), ink (fountain pen not ball-point), and colour (preferably unusual, eg., green or brown, not black or blue). Spacing is also important — wastage is a critical feature. There should be an ostentatious disregard for the cost of paper and large amounts of blank paper conspicuously unused are desirable.

The *letter* then is frequently chosen as a medium for communication not purely from the perspective of economy and efficiency, but rather because it has other more psychological advantages. The *telephone* offers numerous advantages over the letter — feedback is immediate (if you get the person in); it has a rather different legal status (ie., there is no record); one can queue jump often quite effectively, unless the person with whom one wishes to speak has a filter mechanism (ie., unhelpful PA).

But the telephone has two other major advantages certainly over the face-to-face meeting. The first is that you may speak to somebody (and they to you) without knowing practically anything about them. That is, what psychological or demographic variables can one recognise from a telephone voice? Sex? Probably, though we have no doubt all made embarrassing mistakes on this issue. Age? Perhaps people under 10 or over 80 years but it is very difficult to make accurate judgements. Education, race? Very unlikely. What about detecting their emotions or whether they are lying? Again, unless at the extremes of anger, fear or depression, it is very difficult to detect a person's mood or indeed their implicit intentions when communicating over the telephone. We have all no doubt experienced surprise at seeing a favourite radio personality on television and finding they are older or younger, balder or more hirsute, plainer or more handsome than one has imagined. Indeed, their looks and shape may account precisely for why they are radio as opposed to television presenters in the first place.

Of course, not knowing much about the person may be advantageous to either party. Just as you cannot know the age, looks, handicaps, etc., of the person you are talking to on the telephone, neither can they know much about you. Hence the use of a telephone voice ... an attempt to present an image through accent and tone of voice that is specious but desirable. In other words, the telephone offers some of the major advantages of face-to-face communication, such as speed of feedback, but crucially offers none of the tell-tale non-verbal cues which allow one to detect how honest, sincere, committed, truthful, etc., is the person with whom we are talking.

The telephone offers one other major advantage though there may be exceptions to the rule. Because one pays for a call in terms of a multiple of time and distance, the average time spent on the telephone is probably considerably shorter than the average time spent face-to-face discussing exactly the same problem. Niceties and trivia are usually reduced and one gets down to the point of the communication far more quickly. People may feel the need to provide refreshments when meeting face-to-face, or may be interrupted by a third party. With the exception of adolescent females, however, telephone calls are fortunately rarely too long and furthermore one has a whole host of possible excuses (lies) why they should be terminated (kettle boiling, knock at the door, etc).

But most people prefer to communicate face-to-face. They need more than verbal (written) and vocal (audio) cues to give and receive complex messages, though of course in doing so they lose some of the advantages of the letter and the telephone outlined above. Academic ethnologists, zoologists and psychologists have tended to agree with the songwriter 'It's not what you say, it's the way that you say it,' so emphasizing the role of non-verbal cues, such as eye gaze patterns, body posture, movements, gestures, and the like in communication. That no doubt is true. The crucial point is the medium you choose to say it through.

➤ People in business choose every day to communicate principally through three media: the written media of letters, memos and notes; the vocal medium of the telephone (internal and external); and the visual medium of the meeting.

➤ Each medium has distinct advantages and disadvantages mainly concerned with what information is not sent, because of channel restrictions, but also subtle attempts to create impressions made possible in certain channels.

➤ The letters regarded by many as old fashioned and inefficient offers many opportunities to communicate without either disclosing too much about oneself or having to deal with immediate feedback.

➤ Equally the disguises possible on the phone, coupled with the need to get on with it, makes it the preferred medium for many business people.

D. Problems with Employee Attendance

Absenteeism, or the non-attendance of employees for scheduled work when they are expected to attend, is a major problem which merits wide attention. In a report published in 1987 by the Confederation of British Industry, it was estimated that absenteeism was costing British companies £5 billion a year. The Director magazine, at this time, commented that 200 million days were lost each year by British industry due to employee absence without leave, while the Industrial Society calculated that the average shop floor worker took 11 days off a year. This, however, is not a national malaise. A 1993 Industrial Society report indicated that Japanese-owned businesses in the UK outperform British-owned companies in attendance rates. The report attributes this to better monitoring and internal communications and to Japanese companies' emphasis on teamwork.

Absence rates in Britain have been falling over recent decades, partly reflecting better management and healthier workforces. But the cost in terms of lost production is still large. Are there further steps to be taken to remedy this situation?

Despite their importance, employee attendance problems represent a topic with which organizations often fail to get to grips. Why should an issue so central to the well-being of any company be so neglected? There are a number of views about this.

first, it may be that organizations are just too embarrassed to address this issue internally, let alone discuss it publicly in management journals. Absence is a very visible sign of employees voting with their feet. Thus, for a company to admit it has an employee attendance problem is perhaps to admit to being perceived as a bad employer.

Second, along with the weather, managers may treat absenteeism as an act of God that has to be endured rather than as an organizational problem capable of being solved. Even if they believe that something can be done about it, there is surprisingly little up to date information on causes and controls of absenteeism available in a form that can be directly used by management.

The existing body of literature on employee absenteeism divides neatly into two parts. The academic research, mainly, though not exclusively, American in origin, addresses itself to the causes of absenteeism and largely ignores the practical question of reducing it. The professional and managerial literature, in contrast, offers endless solutions, generally based on an account of what one or two companies have done. The reported success deals exclusively with what management did, but fails to discuss either the possible causes of absenteeism in that particular company, or whether the chosen solution is appropriate for other organizations operating in different circumstances.

In the UK, CBI research has shown that similar companies in the same industry, in the same locality and with equivalent workforces, can have astonishingly different levels of absenteeism. Some firms have absence levels one-fifth of their local competitors. The practical experience of companies shows that it is possible to achieve substantial improvements in attendance levels. The means of improving attendance lie in the hands of the employers themselves.

Research has repeatedly shown that levels of absenteeism differ greatly between companies. Experience has shown that management can take positive steps which can greatly reduce levels of absence. Attendance can be managed. According to the CBI, however, there is no single strategy for improving attendance. Different approaches work in different circumstances. There are also different levels of approach, starting from accurate monitoring and control, through mechanisms for fostering employee commitment to the positive promotion of good health.

People cannot be expected to fall sick only at weekends or during holidays. Moreover, one worker's time off for flu is another's escape from infection. It could be argued that tolerance of reasonable absenteeism — even allowing workers occasional mental health days — is a goodwill investment and an insurance against abuse.

This kind of regime can only operate beneficially if there is a high degree of trust and shared awareness between employers and staff. On this count, British companies do not score highly. Absence is, for many, a forgotten problem. Records are rudimentary, communication of attendance data is negligible and control measures are crude and ill-focused. For these reasons, getting a grip on absenteeism can yield substantial savings.

Accurate records and monitoring are the essential foundation for an attendance management policy. Such information is needed to allow companies to review their overall performance against internal and external measures and to ensure that prompt action is taken at the individual level when an employee has a poor attendance record.

The starting point of any system of attendance or absenteeism management must be to define what it is that is being monitored and reviewed. A business needs to have data which provide a clear picture of how it fares overall with regard to attendance, to aid planning any appropriate corrective action. Accurate statistics will allow companies between different sites, different departments, different work groups and so on to plot these differences.

Calculating absenteeism needs to take into account not just crude percentage time lost but also the number of separate absence spells.

There is a world of difference when it comes to corporate efficiency between one worker being absent for five working days and five workers each taking one day off. Most firms' records are incapable of making the distinction. Simple computerized recording systems are widely available which can provide this and other breakdowns.

Employers need to consider both the type of information that should be gathered and the way in which it should be presented. Lessons learned by various companies have been listed by the CBI in the UK. first, the information provided should give some idea of overall non-attendance levels in the company or establishment as a whole. The records need to be clearly defined so that, for example, non-attendance due to sickness cannot be confused with non-attendance due to industrial action or other causes. Second, differentiation should be made between long-term and short-term absence as they require different treatment. Third, it is useful to look at statistics over a rolling twelve month period in order to assess whether attendance levels are deteriorating or improving and the extent of annual, seasonal and weekly trends.

A further management technique is to provide attendance incentives. Most corporate thinking about this is limited to a carrot and stick approach — often with more stick than carrot. Both elements are important. The use of punitive measures only, without positive incentives, can result in aggregate absenteeism levels getting worse, not better. Really bad offenders may reduce their absenteeism rates, while mild offenders may become much worse than usual.

For many companies, attendance incentives tend to be thought of in terms of material rewards. But this can raise further problems. Management may be quite understandably reluctant to give staff additional rewards simply for fulfilling the basic terms of their employment contract, ie., putting in an agreed number of hours work attendance each week. Furthermore, staff unlucky enough to fall genuinely ill may feel harshly treated if they lose an attendance bonus as a result.

Research has shown that the most effective incentive carries almost no cost. It is recognition. Good absence information systems raise awareness of attendance performance. The most effective distinction here is a shared awareness of attributable costs.

Attendance-motivated workers are found in companies where individuals are aware of how their absence affects group performance, with the implicit sanction of group disapproval for absence. This is only likely to occur where groups are interdependent enough for individual behaviour to be visible.

finally, do illness and stress relate to absenteeism? Multiple factors have been identified as underlying and contributing towards absenteeism. These various factors reside within individuals and in the organizations that employ them. According to the Industrial Society, illness and stress are prime and interconnected causes of employee absenteeism. Employees are more likely to become ill when bored, unhappy and demoralised.

Absence has two interacting causes: risk and susceptibility. These factors are related to the two key mechanisms affecting absenteeism, the *motivation* of employees to go to work and their *ability* to do so. An unhealthy life style is a risk factor and low morale a susceptibility factor. The highest rates of absenteeism are found among young and low status workers. They are at risk through their lifestyle, which affects their ability to turn up to work, and their status means that they are more likely to take time off because of low attachment to the job.

Absenteeism can be reduced where risk factors are minimized through careful hiring policy and preventive health programmes, and susceptibility is reduced through enhanced trust.

➤ Absenteeism costs industry billions of pounds every year. Despite its importance, it represents a problem many organizations fail to get under control.

➤ Employee attendance can and does often need to be managed. It is essential to distinguish genuine illnesses and absences from the kind of malingering which justifies much self-referred periods off work.

➤ Companies must keep accurate records and implement a comprehensive monitoring system. They are essential foundations for an effective attendance management policy.

➤ Counting up points of absence needs to be taken into account not simply the overall amount of time left, but the number of separate spells.

➤ Attendance incentives can be effective. The best schemes are not necessarily the most costly. Often the most effective way of encouraging good attendance is recognition of employee performance.

➤ Corporate health and safety audits can play an important role, by encouraging lifestyles and working procedures designed to enhance the health of employees and encourage commitment and motivation to attend.

6
TEAMWORK

Despite the fact that many managers pride themselves on their rugged individualism, few can overlook the fact that they work in teams. Not all managers are fortunate enough to choose their own team — often they may inherit or get assigned to them the team they work with.

Working in teams can be a cause of both joy and frustration. Team spirit can be good, bad or indifferent, but it is not always clear whether it is a cause or consequence of team effectiveness.

Teams also hide 'social loafers' — those who do nothing when with others. They are in part responsible for why teams often do less work than would occur if individuals worked alone.

"I'm beginning to suspect you're just not a team player, Stapelton"

A. Working in Teams

Nearly all of us work with other people. Most of us are interdependent in the sense that we have to help, support and reward each other at work. No one can whistle a symphony; it takes the team effort of an orchestra to play it. Whether we call them groups, sections, squads or teams, most of us realize how much our work productivity and satisfaction is due to them. This pretty obvious point is now the latest management obsession.

Management science, if there can be such a thing, is notoriously faddish. Not long ago it was strategic planning that was the key to organizational success. Then, the spotlight turned on organization structure. After that the gurus said that once the corporate culture was right, Eldorado was just around the corner!

These solve-all solutions have now reached their sell-by date. But there is, it seems, a new solution to all the hard-pressed manager's needs, namely, teamwork. This will solve all your problems and lead to happy, healthy, productive workers. So business sections of bookshops bulge with tomes on teams and teamwork. They rejoice under crypto-sporting titles such as 'Team Power'; 'How to be a Team Player'; 'Winning Big'. Their message is simple: the power of the waterfall is nothing but a lot of drips working together. No matter how great a warrior he might be, a chief cannot do battle without his indians.

What supporters of the team concept argue is this: bearing in mind that management is the art of getting things done through people, you need to let your people know what your goals are — what you want to accomplish, how you want to accomplish it, how they will benefit from it and the role they will play in accomplishing it. This is another way of saying that the members of the management team must be able to identify themselves individually with the company's overall goals. No chief executive or top management group ever reached these goals by themselves. Unless the entire management team is aboard, the company will never get there.

What has caused this explosion in restating the obvious? The answer is partly in the fearful American obsession with the Japanese. The post-war Japanese industrial miracle has brought particular emphasis to the significance of team work.

The Japanese come from a collectivist culture and hence naturally do things in groups or teams. We, in the Anglo-Saxon world, come from an individualistic culture, which selects for rewards and values individual effort. No matter how much teamwork achieves in our culture, the results

126

tend to get identified with a single name. We therefore have to endure various mildly humiliating training courses (many in the great outdoors) to encourage teamwork because it is not natural to us. While it is true that no member of a boat crew is praised for the individuality of rowing, this is an exception to the rule. The Japanese, presumably, don't feel obligated to attend individualism courses to learn how to become their own person, or do things their own way. They are natural collectivist team players.

This individualism in our culture runs deep. We are, however, loyal to some groups: usually those we have been forced to join, or with whom we have endured hardship and difficulty. The family, school class-mates, or fellow military conscripts do often command our loyalty. But, because we don't have jobs for life and find it easier to get promotion by moving between organizations, we rarely stay long enough in a team to be really part of it.

The life of a team goes through various stages: forming (the getting together); storming (arguing over who does what, who is leader, etc); norming (the acceptance of explicit and implicit rules); performing (actually working well after the early stages have occurred). Teams also go through mourning when they break up. But all this takes time and many of us never really stay long enough in a particular team to appreciate its worth.

But how seriously do companies who have swallowed the team solution really take the idea? Yes, they do talk it up; go on endless (and expensive) courses; even partly restructure sections into new teams. Yet very, very few reward the team, rather than the individual. Most performance management systems (the euphemism for how pay is determined) are explicitly geared to the individual. Yes, teamwork in the sense of contribution to the team may be a criterion which is rated, but it is usually only one of many. Also, we rarely hire people with a team in mind or indeed hire whole teams.

Michael Winner got it right when he said: 'Team effort is a lot of people doing what I say'.

The team work philosophy of cooperation, interdependence and group loyalty is counter-cultural. Our business heroes in the west are for the most part egocentric, rugged individuals, not team players. Team work may be a really good idea, but don't bluff yourself either that it is a total solution or that a couple of fuzzy warm courses will do the trick.

> ➤ Teamwork has become a hot issue in management thinking.
>
> ➤ The move towards team-based activity runs counter to the strong individualism which permeates western management style.
>
> ➤ Team development can be effectively achieved through carefully implemented stages to the benefit of employees and organizational performance.

B. How Important is Team Spirit?

Team spirit and the effective management of work teams can be a key factor underlying success in business. Different managers have different approaches to encouraging and maintaining teamwork. finding a winning combination of individuals who are capable in their own right, but also able to work together effectively, can take a great deal of time and effort. Although luck may play a part in assembling the right group of people to work together, effective teamwork, to a significant extent, grows out of skilled management practice.

Management research has begun to identify the characteristics of high performing managerial teams. From this important work, techniques are being developed to enable managers to learn the key skills essential to improving the performance of the employees under their area of responsibility.

Studies of organizational behaviour have repeatedly shown that many managers do not have a clear understanding of the principles governing high performance teams. The necessary skills can, however, be learnt and integrated into routine management practice. A number of key features are known to characterize the high performing teams.

For a team to work effectively together it is important that its members understand their own personal strengths and how they can work together. To do this, team members need a working model of the key aspects of team management. This provides the basis for self-insight as well as teamwork.

At the heart of every team is the linking function. The successful manager will develop the ability to co-ordinate and integrate the work of other people. Managers who fail to do so will find that their team will not perform at a high level and will gradually disintegrate into a series of individual activities. Managers who have the ability to link and integrate may not necessarily be the most brilliant members of the team. Indeed, they tend more often to be good all-rounders. Their key skill lies in bringing out the best in other people.

Good team managers are good at setting plans and getting other people involved in discussing them and being committed to them. They are good at allocating work to the right people and counselling and advising them as they do it. They are also effective at representing the team and ensuring that it has the necessary resources to fulfil its tasks. A key aspect of this is ensuring that the team members feel that they are being aptly rewarded. The team leader's role in securing these rewards may be more significant in gaining the respect of team members than any nominated position of authority.

Linking is done in various ways. Management by walking about is one method. This brings the manager into regular contact with team members, and not always in a purely formal sense. A more formal aspect of linking is through various staff meetings and committees. The high performance manager will usually ensure that both types of method are used (but not overused) as and when necessary. Some meetings will be necessary, to draw threads together and ensure that action is being progressed. However, more informal linking can be done to bring people together to generate ideas and develop new approaches. Managers of high performing teams often use informal gatherings such as tea or coffee breaks, lunch time chats, or even special social gatherings, to achieve the linking and integrating function of their job. It is more of a word here, or a comment there, combined with the willingness to listen and make suggestions that moves the managerial task along, rather than any specific instructions or memos.

There are 11 principles which characterise a good Linker:

1 Listen before deciding;

2 Keep team members up to date on a regular basis;

3 Be available and responsive to people's problems;

4 Develop a balanced team of individuals with a blend of specialist and generalist skills, who can provide input, advice, organize, take control and introduce new ideas and initiatives;

5 Allocate work to people based on their capabilities;

6 Encourage respect and understanding amongst team members;

7 Delegate work which it is not essential for you to do;

8 Set an example and agree high quality standards with the team;

9 Set achievable targets for the team but always press them for improved performance;

10 Co-ordinate and represent team members;

11 Involve team members in the problem solving of key issues.

Alongside the linking function, there are four major activities which a high performing team will ensure are achieved on a regular basis. In any team, there need to be certain roles which are advisory and others which are more concerned with organizing.

The advisory role in a team invariably relates to gathering information, planning and the creation of ideas. At the opposite end is the organizing function which concentrates more on implementation of decisions, the setting up of systems and procedures, and the establishment of time deadlines, with the emphasis on action. Some people prefer to stand back and take more time and will therefore usually prefer more of an advisory role.

Another aspect of any active team relates to the behaviour that people engage in. Here there are two key behaviours. There are those people who prefer to be 'controllers' and who put a heavy emphasis on setting standards, detailing specifications, achieving outputs in a neat and orderly way. Essentially they make sure that the team works according to a pre-set plan of action. And then, there are 'explorers' who often like to go beyond the status quo. They enjoy looking for new opportunities and bringing new ways of doing things into the organization. The challenge to explorers is to change the way things are done, rather than just reproduce the traditional pattern of working. This, of course, may conflict from time to time with those people who wish to control things in an orderly and well-established way. Depending upon how they are managed the tension between these two types of team member may be beneficial or destructive in relation to performance.

Any high performing team will therefore have to skilfully manage the interface between the advisory and the organizing function and the exploring and controlling forms of behaviour.

The work that has been done on high performance teams indicates that it is possible to measure the individual members' work preferences and the way they will work together as a team. In this way, it is possible to ensure that balanced teams are formed. Moreover, the measurement of such individual work patterns provides the basis for the manager to bring the team together to discuss how they can improve their performance.

A central aspect of developing any team is to have a thorough understanding of the work roles that are required. No one person can do all of the work in a team. Indeed, that is the reason for having a team in the first place, so that the work can be shared rather than falling on one person. The task of the manager is to make sure that the members of the team operate according to their individual strengths, and have co-ordinated rather than unbalanced workloads, with some people having far too much to do and others with too little.

➤ Team spirit has been identified as a key factor underlying management success.

➤ For teams to work effectively, their members must understand their own strengths. Managers must know how to link the various roles and functions the team is to perform.

➤ Clear definition of roles within the team, for example, the advisers and organizers, is key to knowing how to integrate their various functions.

C. Social Loafing: Why Team Work Can Produce Poor Performers

Teamwork is one of the latest fashionable concepts in management science. Creating healthy integrated teams of workers is thought to boost company morale and performance. There is, however, a downside to placing people in teams which is often overlooked. It derives from a behavioural phenomenon which psychologists have known about for a long time.

When people know that their work will be combined with that of others, an interesting thing often happens: they don't work as hard as they normally would when on their own. Instead they may be tempted to let others do their work for them, while just going along for the ride. Although a group of people might be expected to be more productive than any one individual, in practice, individuals may work less hard in the company of others than when on their own.

This effect was first noted over 50 years by a German scientist named Ringleman, who compared the amount of force exerted by different size groups of people pulling on a rope. Specifically, he found that one person pulling on a rope alone exerted an average of 63 kilogrammes of force. However, in groups of three, the force per person dropped to 53 kilogrammes, and in groups of eight it was reduced to only 31 kilogrammes per person - less than half the effort exerted by people working alone. In short, the greater the number of people working together on the task, the less effort each one put forth — an effect known as social loafing.

The phenomenon has been studied extensively by American social psychologist Bob Latané and his associates. In one of their earliest experiments, groups of students were asked to perform a very simple task — to clap and cheer as loudly as they could. The participants were told that the experimenter was interested in seeing how much noise people could make in social settings. Comparisons were made between the amount of noise produced by one person relative to groups of two and six people. Although more people made more noise, the amount of noise made per person dropped dramatically as the group size increased. Pairs of people made 82 per cent as much noise as individuals on their own and groups of six produced only 74 per cent as much noise.

The phenomenon has been explained by social impact theory. According to this theory, the impact of any social force acting on a group is divided equally among its members. The larger the size of the group, the less is the impact of the force on any one member. In the study just described, the participants faced external pressure to make as much noise as possible. With more people present, there was less pressure on each separate person to perform well. The responsibility for doing the job was diffused over more people when the size of the group increased. As a result, each group member felt less responsible for behaving appropriately, and social loafing occurred.

It is not only physical effort that is affected by the social loafing phenomenon. Mental effort can also be reduced when people believe their judgements are being combined with those of others. In another investigation individuals were asked to make a series of assessments of fictional applicants for a job. Participants were told either that they were the only one responsible for making these assessments or that their assessments would be one of two, or one of sixteen, that would be combined to make the final job evaluations.

Once again, the social loafing phenomenon occurred. Assessors made less complex and thorough judgements about candidates when they believed that others' judgements would be taken into account in addition to their own.

These findings are valuable because they show that the social loafing phenomenon occurs when people perform mental as well as physical tasks. Further evidence has shown that when participants believe they are part of a large group performing a particular task, they perceive their own performance to be less significant and therefore more dispensable than when they are operating on their own or as part of a very small team. When working in a large team, people may report feeling that their own contributions are a waste of time, or are likely anyway to be duplicated by the efforts of others. As a result, they put less effort into their own work.

Thus, social loafing may occur because people believe that their contributions to a joint effort involving many others are needed less than they would be if the same task was performed without the input of others. Reduced effort, therefore, may not be simply explained away as people wanting a free ride. It could be the result of a genuine belief that one's contributions are unnecessary and not very important.

Given that many employees perform their jobs in large groups, it is important to realise that they may reduce their efforts simply because the size of the group makes them feel dispensable. Accordingly, managers need to be sensitive to this possibility and consider it carefully before assuming that a poorly performing employee is lazy — especially one working in a large group. Reduced effort on the part of some employees may simply be the result of their feeling that the size of their work group renders their contributions less necessary.

Obviously, the tendency for people to reduce their effort when working with others could be a serious problem in organizations. Fortunately, there are ways of combating or overcoming social loafing.

One possible antidote seems to be to make each performer identifiable. If social loafing occurs when people feel they can get away with taking it easy — namely under conditions in which each worker's inputs are not identified — identifying each person's performance has proven an effective way of countering social loafing.

Another way of overcoming social loafing is by making work tasks more involving. Recent research has revealed that workers are unlikely to go along for a free ride when the task they are performing is believed to be highly involving and important.

To help in this regard, it has been suggested that managers should reward individuals for contributing to their group's performance. Instead of the usual practice of rewarding employees for their individual performance, rewarding them for their contributions to a group effort may help them focus on collective concerns and less on individualistic concerns. In so doing, employees would be expected to become more sensitive to the overall performance of their work groups. This is important, of course, in that the success of an organization is more likely to be influenced by the collective efforts of groups than by the individual contributions of any one member.

> Teams don't always bring out the best in people.

> The larger the team the greater the likelihood that individual members will reduce their personal work effort — social loafing.

> Managers need to beware of this phenomenon and take steps to reduce its occurrence: by making individual performance identifiable; making work tasks more involving; and rewarding individuals for their contribution to team performance.

D. Can Team Spirit Go Too Far?

A healthy team spirit can work wonders for employee morale and performance. Such spiritp is often underpinned by the degree of cohesiveness within any group of individuals who work together towards a common purpose.

Cohesiveness, as such, can be defined as the pressures team members face to remain a part of their group. Highly cohesive work teams are ones in which the members are strongly attracted to each other, accept the team's goals, and help work towards meeting them. In teams which lack any semblance of cohesion, the members may dislike each other and may even work at cross purposes.

Several important factors have been shown to influence the extent to which team members tend to stick together. One such factor involves the severity of initiation into the team. Research has shown that the greater the difficulty people overcome to become a member of a group, the more cohesive the group will be.

Team cohesion also tends to be strengthened under conditions of high external threat or competition. When workers face a common enemy, they tend to be drawn together. Such cohesion not only makes workers feel safer and better protected, but also encourages them to work closely together and coordinate their efforts in combating the common enemy. Under such conditions, petty disagreements that may have caused dissension within teams tend to be put aside so that a co-ordinated attack on the enemy can be mobilised.

Highly cohesive teams, however, can have benefits and drawbacks. The consequences of cohesiveness are not always positive.

On the positive side, it is known that people enjoy belonging to a highly cohesive team. Members of closely knit work groups participate more fully in their team's activities, more readily accept their team's goals, and are absent from their jobs less often than members of less cohesive teams. Not surprisingly, cohesive teams tend to work together quite well and are often exceptionally productive. Their willingness to work together and conform to the team's norms is often considered responsible for their success.

Too much cohesiveness in a team, however, may be a dangerous thing. When members of a team develop a very strong sense of belonging and oneness of purpose, they sometimes become so concerned about not disrupting the like-mindedness of the team that they become reluctant to challenge any of the team's decisions. When this happens, team members tend to isolate themselves from outside information, and will reject all and any criticisms of the team's decision and performance. This phenomenon has been referred to as groupthink and can lead to poor judgement and decision making.

The concept of groupthink was proposed initially by social psychologist Irving Janis as an attempt to explain the ineffective decisions made by US government officials that led to such fiascos as the Bay of Pigs invasion in Cuba and the Vietnam war. Analyses of these cases have revealed that the US president's advisers actually discouraged more effective decision making in each case. More recent analyses of the business policies of such large US corporations as Lockheed and Chrysler have suggested that it was the failure of top management teams to respond to changing market conditions that led them to the brink of disaster.

The problem is that members of very cohesive work teams may have greater confidence in their team's decisions than in their own doubts about these actions. As a result, they may suspend their own critical thinking in favour of conforming to the team. When team members become fiercely loyal to each other they may ignore potentially useful information from other sources that challenges the team's decisions. The result of this process is that the team's decisions may be completely uninformed, irrational, or even immoral.

There are a number of recommended strategies for combating groupthink.

1 *Promote open inquiry.* Groupthink arises in response to group members' reluctance to rock the boat. Organization or team leaders should encourage members to be sceptical of all solutions and to avoid reaching premature agreements. It sometimes helps to play the role of devil's advocate; that is, to intentionally find fault with a proposed solution. Although leaders should not be argumentative, raising a non-threatening question to force discussion of both sides of an issue can help.

2 *Use subgroups.* Because the decisions made by any one group may be the result of groupthink, basing decisions on the recommendations of two groups is a useful check. If the two groups disagree, a spirited discussion of their differences is likely to raise important issues. However, if the two groups agree, you can be relatively confident that they are not both the result of groupthink.

3 *Admit shortcomings.* When groupthink occurs, group members are very confident that they are doing the right thing. Such feelings of perfection discourage people from considering opposing information. However, if an organization or team members acknowledge some of the flaws and limitations of their decisions, they may be more open to corrective influences. Try to keep in mind that no decision is perfect. Asking others to point out their

misgivings about a team's decisions may help avoid the illusion of perfection that contributes to groupthink.

4 *Hold second-chance meetings.* Before implementing any decision, it may be a good idea to hold a second-chance meeting during which group members are asked to express any doubts and propose any new ideas they may have. As people get tired of working on problems they may hastily reach agreement on a solution. A second-chance meeting can be useful to see if the solution still seems as good after sleeping on it.

➤ A healthy team spirit is generally believed to promote work performance.

➤ Excessive cohesiveness, however, can be as damaging as lack of team spirit.

➤ Highly cohesive teams may exhibit good morale and enjoy working together. Equally, there may be a reluctance to challenge team decisions, even when they are unwise or wrong.

➤ This groupthink mentality can be controlled and reversed by promoting more openness of thought before reaching final decisions, by splitting the team into sub-groups designated to tackle independently different aspects of a problem, admitting shortcomings in strategy or decisions via members prepared or appointed to play devil's advocate, and by holding second-chance meetings to reconsider a decision.

7
CORPORATE ISSUES

Many corporate issues have become popular sources of debate and discussion. Developments in management science and economic changes have led topics like corporate culture, business ethics and corporate location to be passionately debated. These are covered in this section along with others like organizational politics and change.

The nature of the organization for which one works definitely has a powerful influence on one's working life. Anyone who has changed job recently will testify to the power of corporate culture and climate!

... and Elsie is our 'Tannic Infusion and General Refreshment Supply Operative!'

A. Corporate Culture

Hermann Goering, Marshal of the Luftwaffe, once said that every time he heard the word 'culture', he reached for his revolver. Some managers might feel the same.

For some time now 'culture' has been a buzz word in management circles. It can be used in two senses. It can refer to ethnic culture — that awfully sensitive issue with a heady mix of racial, language, and religious differences. There is a whole industry dedicated to keeping this issue alive, and in the forefront of people's minds. Just as the past is another country where people do things differently, so cultural differences reflect different ways of seeing, thinking and behaving. Anyone who has worked abroad knows that ethnic and racial differences do matter because they shape how people behave at work.

The second sort of culture is corporate, and it is this which is now the flavour of the month. Managers have found in this amorphous and vague concept an excuse or explanation for their woes but also, often naïvely, a source of hope for a quick fix.

Academic management researchers ask questions about the aetiology, meaning, correlates or indeed even the existence of corporate culture. Populist writers or speakers have more catching phrases and models to describe culture. Thus, some say 'it's the way we do things around here' while others rely more on concepts like values or beliefs for defining culture. Many observers offer appealing typologies of corporate culture that help managers to 'box' or identify different corporate cultures.

Most ordinary people confront corporate culture directly, and somewhat confusingly, only when they change jobs. It is striking how people become so socialized into distinct patterns of dress, language, time-keeping and behaviour in different organizations. Consultants often rely on very subtle cues to understand an organization's culture: the logo, job titles, the company's building, particularly the reception area, and the attire of the MD! The longer one stays in an organization and the less one visits other organizations, the less one notices the unsaid assumptions that dictate behaviour at work. Hence its very existence and power to motivate people is most frequently asserted by those who are frequent job or department changers.

But being faced with a new and different corporate culture can present employees with tremendous problems, as some multi-nationals know to their cost. Large corporations often try to impose a unified, homogenized corporate culture across ethnic or national culture boundaries. Others attempt to

140

'When in Rome do as the Romans do', even though they might draw a line at nepotism, corruption, and inefficiency that they perceive in some cultures.

The reaction to these differences often causes culture shock and managers deal with this syndrome in different ways. Whether it is corporate culture or ethnic culture shock, the results and reactions are much the same.

Discovering cultural differences (whether they are ethnic, gender, religious or linguistically based) is frequently an unpleasant experience. The reactions it induces vary considerably, but people tend to fall into one of the various groups detailed below:

● **Chauvinistic Imperialists:** 'Ours is the best way and others should learn our ways; differences are anyway fairly minimal and due solely to their ignorance.' This approach argues that 'we' have the secret to ethnic and corporate culture, and that the sooner others learn our ways and our language, the better. Love us or leave us is the motto of the chauvinists who, believing they are right and superior, like to impose their way of doing things.

● **Ashamed Post-Colonialists:** 'Theirs is the best, most natural way: and ours is the worst, most exploitative way. Others have the solution. We are, or were, arrogant and wrong.' This rather self-effacing approach seems to be more and more common, especially among those who have lived and worked in an economically declining country or company. After reading or hearing a persuasive management guru some naïve managers attempt a dramatic and immediate culture change, in the hope that it will save them and their business. Being both impossible and inappropriate it nearly always ends in tears.

● **Ignoramuses:** 'Cultural differences don't really exist and are emphasized by people who have ulterior (political) motives.' Here ignorance is bliss. Like the person who believes everyone else has an accent but them, these managers are completely unaware of the powerful cultural forces that shape their business.

● **Relativists:** 'Every culture does things differently and has its share of the truth. Nearly every aspect of culture varies and cultures are essentially incomparable.' Relativists feel rather overwhelmed by the whole business of culture and can find no way of making judgements about culture. They believe that culture can be 'tweaked' and that an adaptive, unique culture can be cobbled together from different sources.

● **Vacillators & Marginals:** 'All cultures are valid in some respects and the trick is to find which has the best answer to the problem. Cultures tend to be completely right or wrong on a specific topic and it is difficult to predict which is which and when.' With this approach, the organization chops and changes in its beliefs and behaviours and is exceedingly capricious. With every new idea some managers attempt to alter their corporate culture to comply with the new demands. This is a nightmare for employees.

● **Mediators:** 'The most sensible approach is to choose the most sensitive, veridical, and appropriate aspects of cultural tradition and attempt to live them out.' This is a sensitive mix rather than a homogenization. Some managers believe in flexibility: in being adaptable and culturally multi-lingual.

● **Hybrid Creators:** 'We should try to create a new hybrid culture that best meets our needs and that is adaptive and healthy.' Creating a culture may be easier said than done. Some managers try to create a new strain of culture that supposedly solves all their problems. But as they discover to their cost creating a new hybrid takes as long as, and is certainly as difficult as, creating a plant or animal hybrid, and frequently the business cannot wait!

Whatever the reaction to corporate or ethnic culture, it remains an issue which will not go away. Human resource experts talk about it the whole time; line managers attempt to change it; CEOs attempt to measure it.

Working abroad often means confronting the heady mix of both ethnic (national) and corporate culture. All kinds of reactions occur: surprise, anxiety, bewilderment, even disgust. After some time, people begin to slot into the above categories, and then cope with the difficulties of being different. If only Goering's revolver could deal with these issues more effectively!

➤ Every organization has a culture that reflects the values, beliefs and behaviours in that company.

➤ Culture takes a long time to be formed and is not easily changed.

➤ Although aspects of corporate culture can be easily observed it may not be clearly apparent what forces maintain patterns of belief and behaviour.

➤ Corporate culture can be measured and described. It is helpful to classify it by various questionnaires which may help understand how it functions.

➤ Managers have powerful and very difficult reactions to being confronted with corporate (or national) cultural issues.

B. Seduced by the Customer Cult

The cult of the customer has become the mantra of today's business gurus. Their chant and cant is: 'If we don't look after our customers, then someone else will'. The faithful respond antiphonally: 'We must always remember that our customers pay our salaries.' Unfortunately, in common with all mantras, this one's strength lies more in its repetition than in its inherent truth.

While it is usually true that successful businesses look after their customers, it is not true that all businesses which look after their customers are successful. Laker Airways looked after its customers with enthusiasm, but went the way of all flesh nonetheless.

A decade ago, the chant was of profit and profitability. Cost centres became profit centres. The high priests were the grey men at the bottom line the auditors who devoted themselves to beating their rewards into profit shares and their careers into catching crooks.

A decade earlier the gospel was of job enrichment and job satisfaction. the belief was that the contented worker would become the affluent worker.

All of these gospels had a kernel of truth but, to correct what they thought were earlier imbalances, the business gurus successively created the imbalances. Gurus and consultants often maintain that what has gone before is fashion, but what they bring is truth. They usually succeed in creating little more than a new fashion.

All businesses will fail in the long term unless they pay adequate attention to the legitimate requirements of their three principal stakeholders: their shareholders, staff and customers.

The shareholders own the business, have invested in it and are concerned that it should be profitable. In this way, the business will produce for them an adequate return on investment, by monitoring and managing their costs and their revenues.

The staff serve the customer and are stewards of the company's resources. The quality of a company's employees is a critical factor in creating business success. Their morale is the indicator of the delicate plant which dies in some, thrives in others and needs constant attention. Its condition needs to be monitored constantly but it is unclear who should carry out the monitoring and how it should be done.

Personnel departments in most businesses need to be involved but they usually fail to provide adequate data to support decision-making about personnel matters. They frequently fail to provide insight into those factors which need to be monitored such as the staff's perception of how they are treated and how that treatment is changing over time.

Ultimately, customers provide profits for the shareholder and salaries for the staff. For too long, customers were neglected, abused or forgotten. Their place in determining the success of businesses has now been restored but it would be inappropriate to concentrate on their needs at the expense of others. Regular monitoring of customer's feelings about the company's products or services can be carried out by market researchers but it is vital to ensure that the data redirected towards decisions which need to be taken rather than meandering into empty description.

For two thousand years, the Christian church has been teaching the difficult concept that God is a trinity — three in one. If there is a God of business, He also has three manifestations: the shareholders, the customers and the staff. They are different, but equal, and all demand similar attention. Those who emphasize the worship of any one over the others are today's false prophets.

> ➤ Never underestimate the importance of customers — external and internal.
>
> ➤ Employees and shareholders are equally important to the welfare of the business.
>
> ➤ Getting the right balance between the needs and rights of customers, employees and shareholders is a manager's primary responsibility.

C. Coping with Organizational Politics

Organizational politics is widespread. Indeed, it is one of the most talked about topics among employers. Internal political machinations don't simply hold an intrinsic fascination for those with an active curiosity and who need always to know what is going on, but can have significant and direct implications for employees' own positions within an organization.

Employees often gain subtle satisfaction out of joining the cynics who relish every opportunity to criticise and question the actions and motives of senior management. This behaviour is not confined to personalities, although anxieties about the way a place is being run usually end up being blamed on particular individuals in the higher positions. Attention may be directed also towards organizational policies in relation to corporate communications, appraisal and development, rewards and career progression opportunities.

Political activity is a part of corporate life. The really important question is not whether it exists, but to what ends is it directed? Do those with political power, whether limited or far-reaching, abuse it?

Given how fundamental the need for power appears to be in business, and how differences in power between employees are basic to organizations, it is safe to say that organizational politics is an (inevitable) corporate fact of life. While this reality must be accepted companies ignore (often negative) effects of organizational politics at their peril. Indeed, lowered corporate morale and diversion from key organizational goals, as employees pay closer attention to planning their attacks on others than to doing their jobs, are expected to result from political activity. In view of this it is critical for managers to consider ways of minimizing the effects of political behaviour. Although it may be impossible to abolish organizational politics, there are several things managers can do to limit its effects.

● **Clarity of job expectations** Political behaviour is nurtured by highly ambiguous conditions. To the extent that managers help reduce uncertainty, they can minimize the likelihood of political behaviour. For example, managers should give very clear, well-defined work assignments. They should also clearly explain how precisely to carry out what employees are supposed to do and what level of performance is acceptable. Under such conditions, recognition will come from meeting job expectations, instead of from less acceptable avenues.

● **Open the communication process** It is difficult for people to try to foster their own goals at the expense of organizational goals whenever the communication process is open to scrutiny by all. Compare, for example, a department manager who makes budget allocation decisions in a highly open fashion (announced to all) and one who makes the same decisions in secret. When decisions are not openly shared and communicated to all, conditions are ideal for unscrupulous individuals to abuse their power. Decisions that can be monitored by all are unlikely to allow any one individual to gain excessive control over desired resources.

● **Be a good role model** It is well established that higher-level personnel set the standards by which lower-level employees operate. As a result, any manager who is openly political in his or her use of power is likely to create a climate in which subordinates behave the same way. Engaging in dirty tricks not only teaches subordinates that such tactics are appropriate, but also that they are the desired way of operating within the organization. Managers will certainly find it difficult to constrain the political actions of their subordinates unless they set a clear example of honest and reasonable treatment of others in their own behaviours.

● **Do not turn a blind eye to game players** Suppose you see one of your subordinates attempting to gain power over another by taking credit for that individual's work. Immediately confront this individual and do not ignore what he did. If the person believes he can get away with it, he will try to do so. What's worse, if he suspects that you are aware of what he did, but didn't do anything about it, you are directly reinforcing his unethical political behaviour — letting him know that he can get away with it.

In conclusion, it is important for practising managers to realize that because power differences are basic to organizations, attempts to gain power advantages through political manoeuvres are to be expected. However, it is a critical aspect of a manager's job to redirect these political activities away from any threats to the integrity of the organization. Whereas it may be unrealistic to expect to eliminate dirty political tricks, minimizing the divisive effects they can have on employees; commitment to and concentration on their work are vital to corporate performance.

> ➤ For most people organizational politics is an annoying and frustrating feature at work.
>
> ➤ Rather than lament its existence, it may be better to cope with it effectively.
>
> ➤ Setting a good example and challenging major players are simple but effective ways of dealing with organizational politics.

D. Business Ethics

Is the current concern with business ethics (a) an ephemeral trend (b) a justifiable pursuit or (c) an oxymoronic impossibility? As business issues, business books and businessmen have caught the popular imagination, so their personal lives, wheeling and dealing and falls from grace have caused scandals.

Recent corporate scandals such as the dirty tricks campaign waged by British Airways against Virgin Atlantic; the Maxwell pension fund fiasco; Ernest Saunders and the Guinness debacle; and Asil Nadir and the Polly Peck saga have provided rich pickings for the gossip columnists and pulp biographers. But those interested in morals and ethics have also been kept busy debating the issues. There is growing awareness of the impact of such revelations on staff morale and on relations with the outside world.

As a response to the current fascination with business ethics, the academics have responded not only with thought-pieces in magazines but also with the establishment of learned journals and even chairs and fellowships at distinguished universities. They run seminars, debate case histories, and even have tests of moral maturity. As a result, the so-called discipline appears to have achieved respectability. Ethics used to be mainly the concern of philosophers and theologians. Some ethicists now venture forth from their abstract, cobwebbed studies into the bright lights and generous free speaking world of the business seminar. Applying Aristotelian ethics to mergers and acquisitions may be something of a problem, but it is a growth business.

In the United States it is estimated that there are over five hundred business ethics courses currently taught on university campuses. There are more than twenty-five textbooks and three academic journals dedicated to the topic. And at least sixteen business ethics research centres have been established. This has produced a bewildering array of sources of advice and guidance, leaving managers concerned that they ought to behave responsibly, but not knowing which brand of moral corporate philosophy they should adopt.

The business world in Britain is also responding to concern about ethical conduct. According to a survey conducted by the Institute of Business Ethics in 1992, thirty per cent of large companies claimed to have a business ethics code and many more were considering adopting one.

Fear of scandal is not the primary consideration. Other surveys have indicated that customers place high importance on the regulation of their suppliers, that employees want to be treated fairly and that shareholders want greater accountability.

In Sweden they take the problem of business ethics seriously enough to have set up a special body to help tackle it. The Institute Against Corruption, which keeps companies up to date about codes of practice and legislative changes, was established in 1923 and is backed by organizations including the Stockholm Chamber of Commerce and the Swedish Federation of Industries. As a result, serious bribery and corruption is unusual in both the public and private sectors.

In Britain, some organizations are beginning to implement their own codes of practice. National Westminster Bank issued a ten page document to more than 90,000 employees during the first half of 1993 which states that the bank's priorities are integrity in its dealings, delivering customer satisfaction and creating opportunities for staff. It also touched on conflict of interest, criminal activities and accepting entertainment 'bribes'.

Other research has found, however, that in many companies there is often a wide gap between professed values and actual behaviour, or at least the public's perception of it. A survey of 119 non-executive directors in Britain by the Ashridge Management Research Group and UK consultancy Integrity Works revealed that there was little consensus about what the term business ethics meant. The majority of respondents felt that business ethics was important, but less than half felt that it was treated as such in practice.

A second study by Helsinki based consultancy Values into Action surveyed 70 senior executives in Britain, the Nordic countries, Europe and beyond. Three in five respondents said they conducted their business activities according to a common set of values. But more than three-quarters of these believed there was a gap between ethical values and actual behaviour, and one in five said that business necessity tended to override such values.

What is ethical as opposed to unethical behaviour? Are political tactics in an organization designed to meet selfish interests only — or will they serve to meet organizational goals as well? Are the interests of others likely to be adversely affected? Under what circumstances does this matter? When do the rights of employees outweigh the rights or needs of the organization? To what extent should employees comply with their employers' wishes?

Ethical dilemmas or choices face organizations all the time. Consider:

Societal Norms		Organizational Norms
Be open and honest	vs	Be secretive and deceitful
Follow the rules at all costs	vs	Do whatever it takes to get the job done
Be cost effective	vs	Use it or lose it
Take responsibility	vs	Pass the buck
Be a team player	vs	Take credit for your own actions

But what is business ethics? It is essentially ethics applied to business issues; it isn't a particular brand of ethics. Thus, one has medical ethics and research ethics. All medical and behavioral scientists are regularly required to subject their research proposals to the scrutiny of the ethics committee. And the same might soon be the lot of the entrepreneur, even the management consultant. Imagine taking every takeover bid, every M & M proposal, indeed each hiring and firing decision to the in-house ethics committee for approval. In a sense we do — many decisions have to be passed by various regulatory bodies which have a quasi-ethical remit. Indeed some business issues are so over-controlled, regulated and monitored there hardly seems any point debating the issues further.

Why have ethics committees been charged with making these decisions? Why can't individuals do it? What training skills or knowledge does one need to be on these committees?

If indeed there is a set of agreed ethical principles to follow, why do we need a committee to puzzle them out? A job creation scheme for the moral majority, perhaps. There are indeed various ethical codes, some absolutist, others relativist, some with general, others with abstract principles. Thus one could mention the radical relativist ethics, called situation ethics, of the American academic fletcher, or the more austere, retributive or absolutist ethics of the Church Fathers or Moslem Clerics. One might ask a trained ethicist or philosopher to fathom out how to apply these abstract ethical principles to everyday business situations, not a jury-type collection of the great and the good.

The real reason committees are used, of course, is to diffuse responsibility. No one person — nor perhaps one moral code — can be held responsible.

A second reason for an ethics committee concerns that bane of American social and corporate life — litigation. Many ethics committees are about 'cover-your-arse' attempts to prevent, circumvent or mitigate legal suits. If this is true, the ethics committee should be replaced by (and renamed) a litigation inquiry.

Rather than waste time and money simply getting 'feel-good' points, a company should first decide on a set of ethical principles (many exist), appoint an expert ethicist to decipher and apply them, and have him/her assisted by a sharp litigation lawyer. Large groups of well-meaning busybodies won't do.

It has been said that if you are guilty, choose to be judged by a jury (which is a committee of the untrained); if innocent, choose a judge and two assessors. The reason is obvious; juries are more likely to make mistakes and be swayed by sweet-talking but obfuscating lawyers. But judges who are trained and experienced are more likely to dispense true justice. Hence, if guilty one has a better chance through the jury making a mistake; if innocent a judge is less likely to be wrong. The amateur business ethics committee, rather than being flavour of the month, has reached its sell-by date.

But there are other ways to uphold a moral code and ensure more ethical behaviour. For instance, chief executives should model and promote ethical standards they approve of. Corporate ethical standards could be brought into many issues like selection, performance appraisal, negotiation with and selection of employees.

More importantly, trained people need to look into specific business ethics questions: is the practice of stonewalling ethical; should the bottom line mentality outweigh human considerations in the work-place; is it acceptable to be less than accurate in corporate advertising?

Deciding on ethical codes and carrying them out is an important issue that is too important (and costly) to be left to a committee of amateurs.

➤ More and more companies are becoming concerned about business ethics.

➤ There is much disagreement in this area but having committees decide is both inefficient and ineffective.

➤ It is important first to try to decide which issues warrant ethical scrutiny and then how the company intends to ensure its ethical standards are followed.

E. Job Title Inflation

We probably have more admirals than ships in the British navy today. Soon, given the exodus of Anglo-Catholics from the Church of England, we might have more bishops than congregations in the established Church. In the unacceptable jargon of politically incorrect speech, most organizations appear to have many more chiefs than Indians.

We might well have monetary inflation under control in Britain, but we could have the start of job title inflation. Most of us have got used to the fact that nearly all Americans over the age of 23 have the title Executive Vice-President embossed on their business card and the trend may be coming here.

These new fangled job titles have elaborate suffixes, usually 'Manager', 'Director' or 'Engineer' if British, and 'President' or 'Officer' if American. Prefixes like 'Senior' 'Executive' or 'Corporate' are also common. Hence one can mix and match any set of these to come up with a grand, but meaningless, job title.

As a result, employees are more concerned about their official titles than their responsibilities. Some ask in interviews 'What will I be called?' more often than 'What will I be doing?'. Hence secretaries, whose job is typing, filing, faxing and coffee making, prefer to be called Assistant Service Directors.

Traditionally 'flat' organizations — those with relatively few levels or grades — such as the Church or the Universities, are being pressurized to invent new titles to keep their ambitious staff happy, while traditionally 'tall' organizations, eg., the army or the civil service, go on inventing new job titles by rendering generalists into specialists however minor the task. There are in fact statistics which suggest that with, say, 15 levels of seniority and the normal span of control (1 to 8 people), one could manage the entire British working population.

Why does this happen? At first glance it seems to many managers a relatively cheap way to reward productivity or service. It's cheap because many people, eager to satisfy their unquenchable self-esteem thirst, are happy to accept an improved job title in lieu of a sizable salary increase. And, it follows, the more problems people have with self confidence and respect, the more they like to compensate with fancy titles. Hence the market for bogus degrees, especially of the PhD variety, allowing individuals to call themselves 'Doctor'. In service industries, people tend to be driven by financial rewards because they are more sensitive to the carrot (reward) than the stick (punishment). The inflationary force of the job title is particularly rife in this sector as a consequence. And because employees are so good at judging themselves and their packaging against others in equivalent companies, once one group starts it there is no stopping this egotistical multiplication of job levels. One airline that has fifty-four levels, including four ranks of tea lady; a bank that has well over thirty levels with nearly a dozen of them known by the handle of 'Manager'; and a hotel chain with well over forty different job titles. Some sectors inflate title grandiosity, but don't increase the number of ranks. This can also be observed in the publishing world where to compensate for relatively low pay (if good expenses) everyone is 'Director' or 'Editor'. But, as with all inflation, there are great dangers to this practice. There is a limit to the number of grand titles that exist; the more they are used, the more worthless they become.

The term Professor in this country is clearly going down that route. It takes time to build up the worth of a job title but not long to destroy it. Despite the imaginativeness of Americans in calling a Personnel Manager the Vice-President of Human Resources it does not help much. Outsiders have no idea what these grand sounding titles are and, like Polish Counts, they are two a penny. The major problem of going down this route, however, is that, far from being a cheap ego trip for staff, it not only becomes very expensive financially, but it raises expectations that cannot, indeed should not, be fulfilled.

Traditionally, job titles prescribed what one did and did not do. Secretaries make tea and type for managers, who may have keys to the executive wash-room, an additional phone or a company car. The title comes with perks. Give employees a fancy new title and they question whether what they do is appropriate for it .

A title is part of a package so it can be very costly. Some companies, in a spirit of crypto-egalitarianism, have chosen to withdraw in-house signs of rank and privilege — the managerial dining room, car park, privilege toilets — while at the same time doubling the number of people with manager, director or some such term in the organization. If everyone is a manager it reduces the worth and the meaning of that title.

Not long ago a British quango had employees with the somewhat demeaning title 'general worker'. Although this term seems more often used in a beehive or an ant colony it endured for many years until job title inflation required it to be changed into 'Chemical Facilitator' or 'Technical Steward' or the like. There are other, better and cheaper ways of rewarding good performance and motivating one's staff than doubling or even tripling the number of levels in an organization or giving everyone (and therefore no one) an impressive and grand title. Some business gurus in fact suggest that the flatter your organization, the fatter your profits. And while inflation may be under control in the economy, it is still rife in the currency of the job title.

But how important is a job title? Does the tendency to make everyone appear on the same job level make a difference — good or bad — to the way an organization runs, to employee commitment or performance? In fact there seems to be a clear trend away from job title differentiation. Indeed, the fashion of de-layering could be seen as a direct response to job-title inflation. There may, however, be a problem with staff who have been used to being rewarded in this way.

The growing tendency towards flatter organizations means either more people with similar job titles or else attempts to find equivalent titles. Whichever occurs, employees will have to get used to bolstering their self-esteem by methods other than fancy job titles. And managers and human resource personnel will have to find alternative methods to reward their ego-hungry staff.

> ➤ Job titles are meant to be logical and informative, but are too often about egotism and obfuscation.
>
> ➤ Managers should learn not to 'reward' staff by giving them meaningless titles just because it appears cheap.
>
> ➤ De-layering means that rather than increasing both the pomposity and variety of titles in fact the opposite needs to become true.

F. How to cope with Organizational Change

Whether it is unplanned and forced, or the consequence of a carefully planned strategic effort, it is almost inevitable that a company will face change at some time during its existence. Change is likely to occur when the people involved believe that the benefits associated with making a change outweigh the costs involved.

The factors contributing to the benefits of making a change are: (a) the amount of dissatisfaction with current conditions, (b) the availability of a desirable alternative, and (c) the existence of a plan for achieving that alternative. Management theorists have claimed that these three factors combine multiplicatively to determine the benefits of making a change.

The implications of this are that if any one of these factors is very low (or zero), then the benefits of making a change, and the likelihood of change itself, are very low (or zero). In other words, people are unlikely to initiate change if they are not at all dissatisfied, or if they don't have a desirable alternative in mind (or any way of attaining that alternative, if they do have one in mind).

Of course, for change to occur, the expected benefits must outweigh the likely costs involved (e.g., disruption, uncertainties, and so on). Professionals in the field of organizational development pay careful attention to these factors before they attempt to initiate any formal, ambitious organizational change programmes. Only when the readiness for change is high will organizational change efforts be successful.

However, the likelihood that any planned attempt at organizational change will be effective depends significantly on the extent to which several formidable barriers to change can be overcome.

Although people may be unhappy with the current state of affairs confronting them within their organization, they may be afraid that any changes will be potentially disruptive and will only make things worse. Indeed, fear of new conditions is quite real; it creates unwillingness to accept change. Resistance to change can originate from both individual and organizational variables.

Several key factors are known to make people resistant to change within organizations.

1 **Economic insecurity** Because any changes to the job have the poten-

tial to threaten one's livelihood — either by loss of job or reduced pay, some degree of resistance to change is inevitable unless job security can be assured.

2 Fear of the unknown It is well accepted that employees derive a sense of security from doing things the same way, knowing who their co-workers will be, and who they are supposed to answer to from day to day. Disrupting these well-established, comfortable, familiar patterns creates unfamiliar conditions, a state of affairs that is often rejected.

3 Threats to social relationships As people continue to work within organizations, they form strong social bonds with their co-workers. Many organizational changes (e.g., reassignment of job responsibilities) threaten the integrity of friendship groups that provide an important source of social rewards for many employees.

4 Habit Jobs that are well learned and become habitual are easy to perform. The prospect of changing the way jobs are done challenges workers to relearn their jobs and to develop new job skills. Doing this is clearly more difficult than continuing to perform the job as it was originally learned.

5 Failure to recognize need for change Unless employees can recognize and fully appreciate the need for changing things in organizations, any vested interests they may have in keeping things the same may easily overpower their willingness to accept change.

As well as these 'people' factors, there are several further organizational factors known to produce resistance to change.

1 Structural inertia. Organizations are designed to promote stability. To the extent that employees are carefully selected and trained to perform certain jobs, and rewarded for performing them, the forces acting on individuals to perform in certain ways are very powerfully determined — that is, jobs have structural inertia. In other words, because jobs are designed to have stability, it is often difficult to overcome the resistance created by the many forces that create the stability.

2 Work group inertia. Inertia to continue performing jobs in a specified way comes not only from the jobs themselves but from the social groups within which many employees work. Because of the development of strong social norms within work groups, potent pressures exist to perform jobs in certain ways, and at certain accepted rates. Introducing changes causes disruption in these established normative expectations, which impose formidable barriers to change.

3 Threats to existing balance of power If changes are made with respect to who is in charge and how things are done, a shift in the balance of power between individuals and organizational sub-units is likely to occur. Those units that now control the resources, have the expertise, and wield the power, may fear losing their advantageous positions as a result of any organizational change.

4 Previous unsuccessful attempts to change Anyone who has lived through a past disaster may be understandably reluctant to endure another attempt at the same thing. Similarly, groups or entire organizations that have been unsuccessful in introducing change in the past may be understandably reluctant to accept further attempts at producing change in the system.

A key factor in making sure that organizational change is for the better is how well change is managed. Given the many sources of resistance to change likely to be encountered, it is imperative that managers attempt to take steps to overcome such barriers. Several useful approaches are known to produce positive results.

1 Shape political dynamics Political variables are crucial when it comes to getting organizational changes accepted. Politically, resistance to change can be overcome by winning the support of the most powerful and influential individuals. Doing so builds a critical internal mass of support for change. Demonstrating clearly that key organizational leaders support the change is an effective way of getting others to go along with it — either because they share the leader's vision, or because they fear the leader's retaliation. Either way, political support for change will facilitate acceptance of change.

2 Educate the work force Sometimes, people are reluctant to change because they fear what the future has in store for them. Fears about economic security, for example, may be easily put to rest by a few reassuring words from senior executives about what organizational changes may mean for them. It is imperative for top management to show a considerable amount of emotional sensitivity. Communicating exactly what organizational change means for the work force can help allay the fears that are a key source of resistance to change. Doing so makes it possible for the people affected by the change to become instrumental in making it work.

Through a process of 'empowerment', employees can be freed from instructions and controls, and allowed to take decisions themselves. This process is increasingly being recognized by academics and consultants as vitally important to make organizations more responsive to the marketplace; to de-layer organizations in order to make them more cost-effective; and to get employees of various disciplines to collaborate together with minimal supervision, by communicating horizontally, rather than vertically up and down the hierarchy.

3 Involve employees in the change efforts It is well established that people who participate in making a decision tend to be more committed to the outcome of the decision than those who are not involved. Accordingly, employees who are involved in responding to unplanned change, or who are made part of the team charged with planning a needed organizational change, may be expected to have very little resistance to change. Organizational changes that are sprung on the work force with little or no warning might be expected to encounter resistance simply as a knee-jerk reaction, until employees have a change to assess how the change affects them. In contrast, employees who are involved in the change process are better positioned to understand the need for change, and are therefore less likely to resist it.

There are varying levels at which employees can become involved in the design and implementation of change.

● **Suggestion involvement** Employees are encouraged to contribute ideas, but their day-to-day work activities do not really change. Under this option, staff are not empowered to implement, only to recommend. McDonald's follows this approach: its Big Mac and Egg McMuffin dishes were both apparently invented by employees, as was a system of wrapping burgers that avoids leaving a thumbprint on the bun.

● **Job involvement** At a somewhat more profound level of empowerment, this option involves extensive job design so that employees use a variety of skills, often in turn. They have considerable freedom in deciding how to do the necessary work. Supervisors need to be reorientated towards supporting the front line or shop floor, rather than directing it. Despite the heightened level of empowerment that it brings, the job involvement approach does not change higher-level strategic decisions about organization structure, power and the allocation of rewards. These remain the responsibility of senior management.

● **High involvement** Under this option, employees become involved not just in how to do their jobs, or how effectively their team performs, but also in the whole organization's performance. Virtually every aspect of the organization is different from that of a control-orientated one. Information on business performance is shared. Employees develop extensive skills in teamwork, problem solving, and business operations. They participate in work unit management decisions. There is profit sharing and employee-ownership. High-involvement organizational designs may be expensive to implement, however. Further, these management techniques are relatively undeveloped and untested. People Express tried to operate as a high involvement airline, and the constant struggle to learn and develop this organizational design contributed to its severe operating problems.

4 Reward constructive behaviours One rather obvious, and quite successful, mechanism for facilitating organizational change is rewarding people for behaving in the desired fashion. Changing organizational operations may necessitate a change in the kinds of behaviours that need to be rewarded by the organization. This is especially critical when an organization is in the transition period of introducing the change. For example, employees who are required to learn to use new equipment should be praised for their successful efforts. Feedback on how well they are doing not only provides a great deal of useful assurance to uncertain employees, but also goes a long way in shaping the desired behaviour.

Although these suggestions may be easier to state than to implement, it is clear that any effort to follow them will be well rewarded. Given the many forces that make employees resistant to change, it is important for managers to keep these guidelines in mind. If organizational change is to be beneficial, it is critical that all employees work towards accepting the change rather than using it as a rallying point around which organizational conflict may focus.

➤ Most organizations face change at some time. Corporate change can be beneficial or harmful depending upon how it is handled.

➤ Change can represent a source of insecurity, threat and anxiety for employees. There may be resistance to change especially if employees perceive that it will not be in their interest or will actually have detrimental consequences for them.

➤ Techniques for promoting positive responses to change include a clear message that the leader is behind it; alleviation of fears for the future by supplying as much information as possible about what comes next; involvement of employees in change efforts; and rewarding constructive behaviour on the part of staff.

G. Corporate Relocation

It is often said that actions speak louder than words. This old adage is traditionally used in reference to the behaviour of individuals, but applies equally well to the actions of organizations. One corporate action to which employees pay particularly close attention is one that has been happening with increasing regularity in recent years — company relocation.

Should a company relocate? Is the upheaval too risky? Or could failing to move represent an even bigger threat to the company's survival? These are key questions which a company's senior management must weigh up carefully before deciding on any move for the organization.

For some companies, there may be little choice but to consider moving to a cheaper or more competitive location. Many businesses, struggling with recession and the pace of change in their markets, are having to re-evaluate how and where they operate. The fierce competition for inward investment between Britain's regions, all claiming to offer first class communication systems, transportation networks, smart new business parks and executive housing, can prove to be highly confusing.

To the people involved, such relocations involve more than just physical changes. When a company moves to a new location, it sends certain messages, not always intended, to the people it employs. Unless company executives take steps to manage and control these messages, they run the risk of unintentionally communicating potentially disruptive ideas about the organization and the role of the employees working within it. The consequences for company morale and performance may be long lasting and survive beyond the move to a new location.

Although companies move for various reasons, employees may not accept these explanations at face value. A major reason for this stems from the inevitable psychological trauma resulting from leaving a safe familiar environment full of memories for a new one.

Employees may suffer not only a fear of the unknown and the uncertainties of a new environment, but even a loss of identity with their old communities — especially when a company has long been associated with a particular city. In response to such upheaval, people tend to seek information that helps them cope with their new situation. How will the move affect their lives?

In the process of searching for such information, employees are likely to find hidden messages in their companies' relocation decisions. Companies move for many reasons — the need for more or less space, to reduce costs, to improve a corporate image, and so on. Although these reasons may be clearly explained to the employees, the trauma of moving may lead them to misinterpret or reinterpret the reasons.

For example, a group which sells off some of its companies will almost certainly need less space. The message to employees will be that the group is reducing size or even going out of business, thereby threatening job security. A company that decides to shift emphasis from its core business and diversify into new areas could need to move to different premises to accommodate such changes. Employees may perceive that the company's goals are changing, creating a great deal of uncertainty and worry about their own future roles within it.

Through any of these kinds of changes, companies may communicate unwanted messages to their employees, undermining confidence and morale. Such interpretations may result in potentially disruptive forms of organizational behaviour. For instance, employees who fear a loss of job security, or simply no longer fitting in, may be tempted to resign in favour of new, more secure jobs. The most skilful and talented employees can be expected to be among the first to go elsewhere, leaving the company depleted in key posts at a time it can least afford to be understaffed in these areas.

What are the lessons that have been learned by companies that have relocated? Are there any tips which can be passed on to organizations in the process of thinking about moving to a new location?

● **Plan ahead — if you can**
In contemplating any move of location, it is important to consider very carefully the kinds of facilities the company is likely to need in the future. This includes facilities on site, in terms of general office or specialized business equipment and services for the comfort of employees. It includes facilities available in the area which will affect how attractive it will appear to employees as a place to live, as well as work. Any relocation can take longer than originally thought and will prove disruptive to business operations. Planning ahead can enable different contingency plans to be set in place to deal with various circumstances which might arise along the way.

● **Key people may quit**
Even when a relocation decision is unanimous among senior management, the reality of it may lead some individuals to reconsider their own positions. When a relocation actually starts to take place, underlying differences of opinion about the way it should be handled may surface which had not been apparent before. A move to a particular location may be seen by some employees as restricting longer term career options. Or once an employee and his/her family have had an opportunity to form an opinion about the area to

which the company has chosen to move, they may decide that they simply don't wish to live there-after all.

● **Don't necessarily move everything**

A decision to relocate doesn't necessarily mean that a company should move everything to its chosen new location. For some businesses there may be advantages to retaining an office at the original location, albeit a smaller one, especially if there is still business to be enjoyed there. Further, a move from a large urban centre such as London, to less expensive provincial premises may make sound economic sense in terms of reducing overheads, but the company must ask if it can still perform effectively from its new location alone. Or could it benefit from retaining an office in a business centre where some of its competition, and more importantly its customers or clients, are still to be found?

● **Moves are about people**

Moving can be stressful not only for the company but for the individuals who work for it. It is important to be generous to key personnel. Avoid creating ill feeling as far as possible. Even managers who are unwilling to relocate may prove to be invaluable in helping to effect the transfer. Paying for house hunting trips can transform attitudes to relocation. It is vital to remember that it affects entire families.

● **A move takes time**

Relocation of the staff of even a modest sized organization may take two years, with shock waves still being felt for even longer.

What else can companies do to alleviate or avoid disruptive reactions from employees? Management researchers have identified a number of steps corporations can take to avoid sending hidden messages.

● **Bring certainty to the situation**

Employees will inevitably have many questions about the new location. What is the community like? What will the new facility look like? Where will the various offices be located? The less employers tell their employees, the more likely employees are to become overly concerned with such matters, leading to stress and lowered performance. It is advisable for management to do everything it can to reduce uncertainty for its workforce, such as arranging pre-move visits, providing assistance in finding employment for spouses, and so on. In short, helping to make the unknown better known is likely to reduce dissatisfaction. What is not communicated to employees may be more unsettling than what is.

● **Keep an eye on employees' feelings about relocation**

It is important to monitor concerns about the move at various points in the process. Some factors may bother people at different times. At first, employees may be most concerned about the personal aspects of the move (giving up their homes, finding new ones, and so on). Later, they may think about how well they will fit in with the company's new plans. Key executives will constantly have to gather feedback from employees about their concerns, and address these concerns with honest, thorough information. Not doing so may undermine the success of the relocation efforts.

● **Make messages constant**
Employees may seek information from several sources, and for the answers to be accepted, they must be the same each time. Hearing one thing from one manager and something completely different from another (which can easily happen given the confusion likely to occur during a relocation) only serves to fuel, rather than reduce, workers' uncertainties, lowering morale even further .

● **Retain some of the old while establishing the new**
Too many changes at once can be overwhelming. Therefore, managers are urged to keep many aspects of the old workplace intact while introducing new ones. It would be unwise, for example, to teach secretaries a new electronic filing system immediately upon their move to new offices. Uncertainty, fear of the unknown, and insecurity may be greatly reduced by introducing one change at a time.

Corporate relocations may represent a tremendous opportunity for new growth and prosperity, both at the organizational and individual levels. But for these benefits to be realized, employers must first become more sensitive to the human side of any geographical relocation of their company, recognizing that moving people is not like moving machines.

➤ Relocation is one of the biggest upheavals an organization can face. It may occur for a variety of sensible business reasons, but can strike fear in the minds of employees and result in wholesale staff resignation.

➤ Employees' anxieties can be reduced by careful planning, keeping them well informed on a regular basis, and providing as much support as possible in enabling employees and their spouses to cope with moving job and home. Certainty must be brought to the situation and patience is required in affording employees ample time to make necessary private arrangements for their families and to overcome the trauma of moving to a new part of the country.

8
CONSULTANCY

Consultants come in many shapes and sizes. They offer help, advice and assistance on a whole range of issues including strategic planning, training and analysis.

This section takes a sideways look at the human resource and the academic consultant. It also considers how to become a consultant.

"When that sign-writer gets back from lunch, he's a dead man!"

A. The Human Resource Consultant

The international growth in the number of Human Resource Consultants (HRCs) over the past decade has been meteoric, if not explosive. Their number is even more impressive if one acknowledges that HRCs go under a fairly large number of status-inflating titles and euphemisms such as 'business psychologist', 'staff development professional', or 'organizational behaviour consultant'. Most often there is a clear inverse relationship between title pomposity and actual competence.

There are many reasons why this American-originated occupation has grown so fast in Britain and Europe and both supply and demand have risen rapidly. HRCs come in many different forms: the entrepreneurial don (usually from a business school); the one man band (often a personnel officer given a golden handshake — or the sack): a small group of like-minded people running a specialized consultancy: or the large, usually international group, offering a wide range of consultancy services.

But what do HRCs do? Why spend up to £2,000 per day getting some outsider into your organization telling you how to run it? Why divulge highly sensitive organizational data to some HRC who might have worked, does or will work for your direct competitors? What have these people to offer? What are their skills?

HRCs offer a number of types of skills, many of which are surprisingly absent from most big organizations' personnel departments. This is mainly because the nature and function of 'personnel' has changed and training is often woefully inadequate. five different and specific skills can be identified as offered by HRCs.

1 Diagnostic.

HRCs can offer a 'second opinion'. They can bring the objectivity and disinterest of the outsider but also the potential experience of having seen the problem before. However, a disadvantage of the diagnostician HRC is that they make their diagnostics in line with their preferred 'skill-solution'. In other words, having a number of expensive solutions (programmes) available, they will force the diagnostics of the problem to fit their products. But a major advantage of using experienced and insightful HRCs is that they can show the organization to be fundamentally flawed in either its own diagnosis of the malady or the proposed solutions. Organizations like to believe that easy solutions are possible; they are also frequently unable to distinguish between explicit and implicit messages from clients, customers or their own

164

staff they meet every day.

For instance, managers' complaints about the number of staff they have in their department to complete work loads could have as much to do with problems in organizational structure, or a particular manager's ambitions, as it does a matter of staffing. Equally, staff complaints about the physical working environment may be more a function of the psychological climate of the office about which they feel uncomfortable or incapable of articulating.

HRCs will tell you that diagnosis is more difficult and important than cure and that therefore getting it right easily merits the 'modest' fee. In this they may be right.

2 Measurement.

Many personnel managers are not highly trained in measuring human performance, abilities, needs or personal preferences (e.g., intelligence, personality, team role preferences). After gullible, but enthusiastic and peer-pressured purchases of flashy but not necessarily valid tests, personnel managers often set about measuring the line-manager's personality or the board's team-role preference. When the only tool you have is a hammer, you tend to treat everything as if it were a nail. Hence organizations measure what they can more frequently than what they need to. And this is where the well-trained HRC can bring to bear a formidable array of well-tested measures. Over 100,000 tests are in print and a good HRC will know where to look for the most appropriate measure.

There is a tendency to use inappropriate tests just because the organization has bought them. Rather than spend all one's effort measuring the personalities of directors, the HRC may wisely recommend the measurement of organizational culture (the values and norms of the organization), the climate (the perception of employees), the communication networks, the clients, the customers or the competitors' perceptions. Organizational problems require organometric audits just like those done by the finance department. Measuring instruments (questionnaires, tests) need to be robust, reliable, valid, multi-dimensional, sensitive to faking, and 'normed' for the appropriate population. HRCs must, of course, not only choose and administer good tests but know how to analyze them appropriately and interpret the data.

As HRCs know, many personnel officers often shy away from objective hard data, preferring softer interviews, reports or selected quotes from 'key players'. This may be one reason why they are often despised by their hard-headed colleagues in accounts, strategic planning and even marketing. Some HRC's are experienced and trained psycho- and organometricians and well able to measure important organizational variables.

3 Instruction

There is, and there will probably always be, a place for 'chalk-and-talk' training. Now more likely to be run with impressive videos, self-instruction and completion booklets, and elaborate feedback reports, the business of education remains a central task of some HRCs. Training adults is a challenging task for the HRC. There are those in organizations who are themselves very bright and highly educated, who may be extremely critical of any outside consultant. Equally, those with chips on their shoulders because they never went to university, or did and did rather badly, may make poor students, flipping between the sycophantic and the cynical. But there are others who are deeply appreciative and very good students.

The good HRC soon realises that training adults is rather different from educating students. Training managers must be practical and concrete with lots of memorable examples and helpful models. Whereas academics are trained to be critical and sceptical, HRC instructors soon realise they are more appreciated if they are enthusiastic and zealous about the cause. HRCs are frequently extraverts with a self confidence that extends somewhat beyond the bounds of their ability. As a result they rarely fear the role of teaching, training or instructing, though they may not be that good at it. Good teaching is a rare combination of intellectual ability and knowing how to put it across.

Certainly, instructing or teaching is a crucial function for many HRCs. For many, alas, the term 'training' has a poor reputation and trainers are considered, rather lowly (paid) sorts of consultant, especially when teachers are trained to deliver 'packaged' courses.

4 Process

Some HRCs specialize in process or interpretation as opposed to product. When, for instance, a management team is underperforming or suffering low morale, the process-oriented HRC might be called in not only for diagnosis but also to cure. Process skills are closely akin to group psychotherapy and indeed that may be how the consultant was originally trained.

Just as most accidents are the result of human error, so quite commonly poor business operations are the result of human frailty. Whether one prefers to use meaningless euphamisms like 'personality clash' or not, many people recognize that the quality of human relationships in offices, teams and departments contributes to business success or failure. It is the intangible psychological factors of morale, conflict and lack of commitment that the process consultant hopes to make manifest and explicit. Good HRCs, and those with psycho-analytic training, are frequently able to reveal unexpected or even paradoxical findings, such as depression amongst employees being a consequence of their anger.

To some, 'process consultants' represent the wackiest California-type psychological air-heads who ask both intrusive and daft questions primarily to embarrass . Furthermore, they may not even come to a conclusion, write a report or deliver any tangible outcome. Insight alone is often the orally explicit goal of the process consultant. It is nearly always the case that process work has to be done by the outside consultant. Politically, the personnel department may wisely judge it necessary to lure in consultants, albeit at some critical (and financial) cost.

5 Systems

Some HRCs are specialists in devising, operating or tweaking systems like a performance management system, selection system or staff development system. More often than not this involves the development of fairly sophisticated computer-based statistical software. As a result, these HRC consultants are not the warm and cuddly process type but hardened fellows.

Because writing software and developing systems is very time consuming these HRCs tend to offer a fairly fixed package. Whilst it is true that it can be personalized or adapted to suit each organization these modifications are usually pretty minimal. In this sense the systems HRC sells packages used by the personnel department.

Some computer illiterate and number-phobic personnel directors are highly gullible to the hard sell of systems HRCs for two reasons. first they may not be able to make an intelligent judgement on either the usefulness, limitations or appropriateness of the system. Second, perhaps more importantly, personnel managers are eager to show that they are up-to-date, 'scientific' and sophisticated and hence impressed by the largely irrelevant packaging rather than the content.

But all organizations need efficient, computer-assisted systems. Some HRC systems experts can devise very useful systems that may last organizations years.

Beware the HRC who claims to be equally competent at each of the above functions. But many business people do recognise that changing a business requires dynamite and it is often the consultant who lights the fuse. Victor Kiam once accused consultants of being like castrated bulls because all they can do is advise, not act. The question, of course, remains where to go to get good advice.

Knowing and understanding what HRC consultants offer and do well is crucial for any company. No 'Which Guide' exists for the naïve shopper, only compendia or lists of companies that specialise in HRC. fitting the consultant to the problem is clearly as relevant as the employee to the job!

➤ Human Resource Consultants offer a number of different services.

➤ It is highly unlikely that one individual, or even a small group (say six or fewer) could offer all the major services required. Based on their own abilities, skills and preferences, individuals tend to specialize and collect around them like-minded others.

➤ Diagnosis, measurement, teaching/training, 'processing' and systems development are the major skills provided by HRCs who can offer extremely helpful consultancy.

➤ Beware the HRC individual or group who maintains they have all these skills; despite protestation to the contrary offers a 'packaged' solution; or offers lists of credentials rather than lists of 'satisfied' clients. It is good business to be all things to all men, but alas something of a pipe dream.

B. The Academic Consultant.

All over the world universities are being coerced into becoming more commercially minded. Other-worldly professors are now encouraged to venture out into the real world and, where appropriate, to sell their skills, knowledge or insight.

Many academics cling to the vision of the university which emphazises the intrinsic value of learning, scholarship and the development of the 'whole person' who seeks knowledge for its own sake. Rather opposed to what they see as the grasping, grubby antics of people 'in-trade', many older dons are fiercely opposed to changes being imposed upon them by government and thence administrative officers in the university. 'But we are different' and 'This is not relevant to us' is frequently murmured in the senior common room.

However, this is not the whole picture. Some academics — particularly those in the applied and medical sciences — have always acted as consultants. Indeed their very reputation often depends on their ability to practise their expertise. But there are also entrepreneurial dons from all disciplines who have tried their hand at consultancy, sometimes in areas quite outside their academic competence. Whilst many dons do the odd book review for a mixture of money, prestige and a reasonable readership, others have set up their own businesses.

The thirst for psychological, behavioural or management consultants seems never to have been stronger. Magazines and newspapers are peppered with attractive looking jobs for psychologists interested in psychological assessment, personal development, management training or corporate change. Most psychological consultants can, it seems, begin straight after graduating and earn nearly as much as their Professors in a couple of years.

But the academic and the business communities are still different worlds inhabited by people with different values, lifestyles and goals. For the businessman, 'academic' means esoteric, inapplicable, in short useless, while for the academic, 'commercial' means exploitative, simple-minded, indeed often wrong. Stereotypes they may be but they exist to the detriment of both parties. But in what respects are the academic and business worlds different? The following table is not meant to be exhaustive, ranked or judgemental. There are no 'four legs good, two legs bad' choices and the dimensions are, of course, simplified. But they may explain some of the problems that members from both worlds have in dealing with one another.

ACADEMIC		CONSULTANCY
Insight and Knowledge	MAJOR AIMS	Action
Low Urgency	TIMESCALE	High Urgency
Elegant	TYPE OF SOLUTION WANTED	Practical
OwnResearch Others' Experience	USUAL SOURCE OF INSIGHT	Others' Research Own Experience
High	LEVEL OF COMPLEXITY	Low
Irrelevant	COST-BENEFIT ANALYSIS	Crucial
Theory backed by data	MEANS OF PERSUASION	Data backed by argument
Written	PREFERRED MEDIUM OF PRESENTATION	Face-to-face
Introvert	PERSONALITY TYPE VALUED	Extravert
Irrelevant	SELF-PRESENTATION	Crucial
Dealt with statistically	DEALING WITH UNCERTAINTY	Dealt with personally

For the academic, the aim of research is to achieve insight, understanding or knowledge that may or may not be useful, applicable or saleable. It is justification enough to know the cause of things and have comprehensive understanding of the issue under investigation. While, for many academics 'pure' research is the major aim of their enterprise, for the businessman research is nearly always applied. Research in most companies is action-oriented, problem-solving. In this sense, the aim is much clearer and probably more short term. Academics start with a puzzle, frequently found in the academic literature which interests or amuses them. It may have no pay-off and be extremely obscure. The consultant has the problem presented to him or her and considers a problem someone is actually experiencing. The former are usually satisfied to know and understand, while the latter want to use knowledge.

It is not just their aims which differentiate these two worlds, but also their methods. Differences will be found with respect to timescales, types of solutions, source of insight, level of complexity and cost-benefit analyses employed.

Consultants are time-conscious, high-urgency people driven by deadlines. They want the answer now and are perplexed by the apparently sluggish, procrastinatory ways of academics. Academics in turn resist the immediate fix-it nature of consultancy. Consultancies certainly adhere to Franklin's

Maxims: 'Lost time is never found again; Remember that time is money'. Expectations about time and its use are indeed a major difference between these worlds. Academic deadlines are in terms of years or months, while consultants work to weekly, daily and even hourly deadlines.

To a large extent, academics and consultants look for different things in solutions to problems. Whereas academics value elegance, parsimony, scope, precision and testability, consultants often value applicability, comprehensibility and feasibility. Academics aspire to create theories and solutions that are clear, logically consistent, explicit, verifiable and systematic. Consultants admire these characteristics, and strive similarly for logical and systematic solutions, but unless the solution is usable, it is near worthless.

Most empirical academics rely on a direct empirical base to support their advice or theories. While the database can be of many kinds, it is important that it is comprehensive, correctly measured and sampled, and free of noise and errors. In this they do not always succeed, but the effort is made (strenuously). Unless clients are willing to invest in some elements of research as part of a consulting assignment, consultants usually have to work with a second-hand empirical base, non-original sources and illustrative case histories to make a point. Where the source of the data may be all-important for the former, it is not for the latter. On the other hand, the 'direct experience' of the academic is frequently second-hand or tangential compared with the really direct experience of the consultant.

The level of complexity of theory, solution or model frequently differentiates the two worlds. Academics' level of analysis is often complex and they expect their audience, whoever that is, to deal with (to understand, make sense of) the complexity. Consultants strive to simplify and clarify to help the audience, the client or the learner to comprehend. Academics are often scathing about consultants' solutions which they regard as simple-minded while the consultant sees the academic as unnecessarily obfuscating on issues that can be presented much more clearly.

Whereas for consultants, and their clients, value for money has always been important, academics are only recently having to argue the potential benefits of their work in relation to its costs. For most academics, cost-benefit analyses are impossible to calculate and they will cite many examples of chance discoveries which have followed from 'blue-sky' research. Consultants have to demonstrate value in the short-term. Solutions have to be found to a satisfactory level in a specified time period. Everything must be 'costed-out'.

Academics rely on the quality of their data or the coherence of their theories to persuade. The numbers do the talking and the ideas speak for themselves. Consultants, on the other hand, often use rhetoric to persuade — an academic, though pre-scientific, technique. This is not to suggest that there are not some extremely skilled academic rhetoricians or that consultants are empirically naïve, but rather to suggest that when looking at their reports and presentations, academics prefer the disinterested nature of extensive empirical data alone, and consultants the power of persuasive words to support the minimal designed and controlled studies. Also these are unusually unavailable to the consultant who has to deal with the world as it exists with all its imbalances. Academics do not provide executive summaries for the hard of thinking or appendices as an optional adjunct. The material is presented in a logical and coherent fashion, and it is up to the reader to make the effort to understand it.

Consultants have to sell ideas, solutions and theories, and they usually prefer to do so face to face. Consultants usually have to be polished presenters with slick slides and helpful hand-outs and their preference is for the live medium. Academics prefer documents, tables, charts and seem happiest giving and receiving information in this cool channel. Not even skilled at chalk-and-talk, most academics feel most secure communicating by writing; hence their new-found love of word-processors but not car phones.

Academics and consultants not only have different personalities but value traits differently. Academics tend to be phlegmatic, stable introverts, respecting and emulating the thoughtful, controlled, reliable, reserved, calm, even-tempered type. Consultants on the other hand tend to be sanguine, stable extraverts — active, impulsive, optimistic, responsive, easy-going and sociable. These differences occur partly out of necessity — consultants have to get on with people, to socialize and to persuade. Academics have to spend long periods alone in libraries and laboratories collecting data very carefully.

To the academic, self-presentation, in terms of dress and equipment, is irrelevant because they value what is being said and the quality of ideas over their packaging. Often shabby, nearly always unfashionable and frequently something of an eye sore, the academic is easy to spot even in a crowd. For the consultant, the precise opposite is true. The consultant never underestimates the packaging of services because he or she has come to learn the extent to which it is influential. In consultancy, first impressions have to be carefully managed since one never has a second chance to create them. Credibility has to be achieved fast.

finally, consultants and academics deal with uncertainty in very different ways. Academics have several ways of having their audiences deal with their uncertainty. They declare any caveats about their study designs and calculate their confidence levels when generalizing results from a study group to the whole population from which the group was selected. Consultants, on the other hand, have to use their best judgement in interpreting partial data, choose the best option for the client, stick their necks out and live with the uncertainty.

There are no doubt hundreds of exceptions to the observations we have described here — instances where the above differences either do not occur or indeed occur in the opposite way to those described. We could only rejoice if the differences did not occur, were minimal or were easily bridged. The problem remains that academics and business people still do not fully understand one another. They come from different cultures, hold different values and expectations, have different aims, personalities and communication strategies.

Those in business would do well to think carefully when choosing those outside their organization who might help them. Certainly, there are both academics who can deal well with the commercial world and consultants whose training and methods are rigorous. But the best advice is still that which underlies all decisions to buy products or services — caveat emptor. Let the buyer not only beware but choose wisely.

➤ For some organizations there is considerable kudos in having a (famous) academic as a consultant. Their acknowledged intelligence, disinterest and wide-reading may be seen as a particularly valuable asset.

➤ Academics and business people live in different worlds. They are chosen, socialized, rewarded and punished according to quite different criteria. The longer they live exclusively in the one or the other world, the less they are able to adapt to understand the needs of, or even interact with, the other.

➤ Major differences lie in the type of data sought to consider problems and solutions; time/money constraints; the way in which information is presented; and the assumptions made about the recipient of the consultant.

➤ The academic consultant may be a double-edged sword particularly if one is unaware of the world from which he or she comes.

C. How to become a Consultant

Consultants, like traffic wardens, are ubiquitous. Years ago there only used to be medical consultants. Then the management consultant became common and now there are fashion consultants, stress consultants and even waste-management consultants.

It seems that from a pecuniary point of view there are two equally desirable titles to attach to one's occupational role. The prefix 'designer' or the suffix 'consultant' seem to be the most popular ways of disclosing one's expertise and simultaneously tripling the fee. Designer jeans or designer kitchens are twice the price of the non-designer equivalent, though to be pedantic both have been 'designed' by someone. But it is usually only 'arty-farty' people who are designers. All others are consultants.

What are consultants? How do they differ from experts, boffins, or advisers? One distinction between an expert and a consultant is that whereas both might be extremely knowledgeable about a particular topic, process or operation, the consultant is expected to be able to communicate that knowledge. Consultants, then, have to be good not only at solving problems (or at least re-defining them) but also in communicating to clients how it was done and which strategy they should then follow. Cynics might argue that the crucial distinction between experts and consultants, is that the former tells you what is popular (in the sense of what the client wants to hear) even though it is untrue. And yet as consultants have often found, honesty is the best policy because there is far less competition.

No area of knowledge, skill or expertise is too small, trivial or mundane to have consultants. The idea of working for oneself, charging large fees and being able to pick and choose from various jobs only the most interesting and lucrative, is indeed appealing. So why not 'go for it' as we now say in the new enterprise Britain and become a consultant. After all, success is just a matter of pluck. Secretaries can become word-processing consultants; cleaners might venture into household hygiene consultancy; while night-watchmen may prefer to be called in as nocturnal security consultants! The following rules of thumb are those obeyed by all astrologers, graphologists and others who are able to convince strangers that they know all about them through their mysterious art and powers. These techniques enable them to persuade even sceptical and intelligent clients that through their technique and expertise they somehow penetrate into the real person and hence know all about them. They are of course tricks, and relatively easy to learn.

Before spelling out these simple but powerful strategies, it is probably wise to assume the following: first that people, bureaucracies and organizations are more alike than different. After all, all organizations have one thing in common; they are all different. Secondly, it should be assumed that most problems are generated by a small number of issues mainly to do with coping with change, problems of misunderstanding and miscommunication between people, and issues concerning motivation. Thirdly, assume that with few exceptions, consultants are called in not only to solve problems and provide unique counter-intuitive and singularly correct solutions to impenetrable problems, but to listen to the moans, groans and conflicts of those seeking their help. Often in the business world the introduction of new ideas, products and processes follows a clearly defined path — wild enthusiasm, disillusionment, total confusion, search for the guilty, promotion of the non-participants and the calling in of a consultant. When committees have failed, consultants are called in. Of course, wise consultants know that it is the function of committees to avoid decisions, not reach them.

Another sound piece of general advice is to aquire a sophisticated, general but always applicable stock-spiel delivered in mid-Atlantic 'new speak' that sets the stage for specific advice. This must be delivered with cultivated sincerity and audio-visual polish. It is not good enough to follow the old strategy of when in doubt mumble, when in trouble delegate, when in charge ponder. One must be fast, articulate and smooth, even though vacuous. What is said, shown and presented is far less important then how it is presented. Style is in!

And now for the general points. How to become a consultant:

● Remember that the key ingredient of consultancy is confidence. It is crucial to look and act as if you know exactly what you are doing, have marshalled all the facts and fully understand the problem even if, as is most likely, you are as baffled, if not more so, than those who hired you. It is your role to give them certainty where none exists, to be *in loco parentis,* to make people feel secure.

● Make creative use of the latest statistical abstracts, polls and surveys, even newspaper reports and columnist speculations. There is awealth of material readily available and totally free which allows one to converse with authority (and statistics) about many relevant topics. A consultant may make correct decisions on the basis of few or no facts but gut-feeling, and has therefore to have some background knowledge. Quality newspaers and business magazines provide one with all the knowledge one needs.

● Set the stage for your presentation. Profess a certain degree of modesty and make no excessive claims while not under-selling yourself. This catches the client off his or her guard and helps produce restrained and therefore possibly realisable expectations. Profess omniscience to get the job but only human frailty while on it. Be sure to make the client feel that it is a collaborative exercise and that if it goes wrong it is equally their fault!

● Gain the co-operation of the client in advance. Argue first that you will talk in general conceptual terms which the client will naturally apply specifically to his organization or problem. This puts the onus on him or her to make the connections, which of course also helps you to find out what is going on.

● Have a high-profile, high-tech look. This refers to dress, briefcase, slides and presentation equipment. It must look expensive, up-to-date and complicated. Any gimmick helps. In fact, well prompted, most clients know both the cause and the solution to their problems! And tell the client that there is only time to discuss certain aspects of the problem or issues arising from it. What is left unsaid may be terribly enticing and give additional credibility.

● Have a list of stock phrases on the tip of the tongue. This refers to common management jargon terms, not specifically from your area of speciality but the sort of things you might hear in well-to-do circles. For instance 'ritzy margins', 'intelligent systems', 'serious money', 'exchange rate mechanism', 'organometric analysis'. Reading popular block-busting books may help provide this necessary jargon.

● Keep your eyes open for the corporate culture. There are signs everywhere from the way you are greeted in organizations to the range and type of extra-mural events available. This will give you a feel for how you should present yourself and your 'solution' to have maximum impact. Note the dress codes of people in the organization; the presence or absence of 'art'; commonly re-occurring phrases or jargon; stories or myths about company heroes; job titles etc. All give crucial clues about the organization.

● fish for what the client wants or knows. Clients may deliberately hold back or unwittingly not tell you important information either to test you or because they did not know that it was important. It may be very relevant so pretend you know it and ask for clarification. Often all you need to get them to do is to think through the problems and discover the solution themselves while you take the credit. Psycho-analysts have practiced this trick for years. They get paid by the hour but their patients do 95 percent of the talking and eventually stumble on both the cause and cure for their problem.

● Learn to be a good listener. Certainly psychiatric, psychological and social work consultants are paid not to say anything but simply listen. It might be boring but it is a very easy way to earn money. Just reflect back what the client says and they can usually keep going for hours. Learn to use their phrases and to ask unusual, possibly intrusive questions.

● Dramatise your presentation. This refers to the multi-media presentation that one gives at the beginning and end of the consultation. All public presentations are drama, not the forum for the exchange of information on complex problems. Many executives can only make judgements about quality, lay-out and colour of slides not their content. It is better to have professionally produced meaningless slides that good ideas presented tackily.

● Always give the impression that you know more than you are saying. This is a very powerful tool which may inspire both confidence and possibly more business. Indeed when all is said and done there is more said than done but make sure your client believes there are things that are not said.

● Don't be afraid to flatter your clients at every opportunity. The ability to get on with clients is the first priority of consultants so make sure they like you. And nearly everybody is a sucker for flattery as long as you find the right approach and topic. Use their name constantly, to tell them that relative to other comparable job holders they are far superior.

● Tell the client what he or she wants to hear. It is not unusual for you to be called in to confirm the existence of rather than to find a solution to a problem. Make sure you know what answer the client has in mind and skilfully give it to them. Remember that you may be a political pawn in a rather big organizational chess game. Make sure you know who the players are!

The most intelligent people are those who know who and when to ask for advice. They know that asking dumb questions is easier than correcting dumb answers.

For many who have been disappointed by their encounters with consultants, 'experience' is all they got when they ended up not getting what they wanted. Indeed, blessed is he who expects nothing or little for he shall not be disappointed.

In general it is easy to set oneself up as a consultant. But the advantage of knowing how it is done enables one also to spot the fakes, 'wide-boys' and 'con-artists'.

➤ The growth-industry in consultants of all sorts is due to both demand and supply.

➤ The pay and life style, but not the stress factors, make the job seem very attractive and many people have been lured by the benefits.

➤ Just as one can learn the art of 'cold reading' used by circus and bogus astrologers, palm-readers, graphologists and the like to persuade naïve clients that one really has an insight into their personality and problems, so one can learn 'cold reading' for consultants.

➤ A cynic or sceptic may observe that some consultants are not all they appear to be and rely for their insights on a series of rather clever tricks. But just as people are helped by bogus '-ologists', so clients can genuinely be helped by untrained consultants.

➤ The moral of the story is beware the tricks of consultants who do not and cannot know as much as they pretend to.

9

BUSINESS ETIQUETTE

Etiquette or modern business manners is fascinating and also important. Etiquette dictates how we should behave and helps to oil the machines of social intercourse.

Much business is done over lunch and it is clearly important to know how to behave — what to eat and drink, how to order etc. The style of the business card is also important and may directly affect the impression one makes. Indeed even choice of briefcase should not be overlooked. This section casts a quizzical eye over the modern manners of those in business.

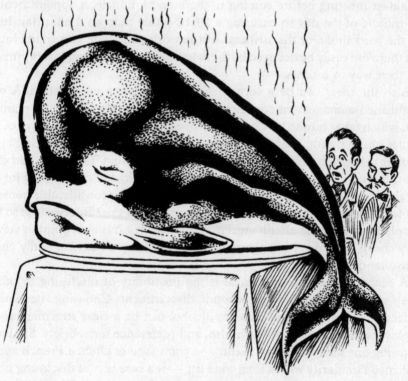

"It might impress our Japanese clients, but if the Green Consumer lobby gets wind of this..."

A. The Business Lunch

Everyone knows that there is no such thing as a free lunch. But still a great amount of business is done over a meal. More and more our European and American entrepreneurs have chosen breakfast as the main business meal. Chic brasseries all over great capital cities echo with mid-Atlantic vowel sounds long before many are capable of socialization alone let negotiation.

But why choose to do business over a meal, be it breakfast, lunch or dinner? What are the advantages of the dining, as opposed to the board room, table? There are many good, if implicit, reasons for people to have a working meal.

It is paradoxical that in many instances the business lunch is cost effective. Being at meal-times, which is traditionally break-time or pre/post work time, one is ensuring that people are working longer hours. They may have a breakfast meeting before coming to work and a luncheon appointment in the middle of the day so ensuring a 10-12 rather than an 8 hour day. Ideal for the workaholic or the advocate of the work ethic! The cost of the lunch can therefore easily be defrayed by the extra hours put in by employers munching their way to success.

Also the meal can be a very cheap way of getting information. A well established management consultant regularly sends the bill to an organization which takes him to lunch in expensive as well as modest restaurants. He argues, quite rightly, that in his capacity as a consultant he was being hired to offer his advice and insight into a technical problem. The client had chosen the venue for the meeting, and although they had of course paid for the meal this had not absolved them from paying a not inconsiderable consultant fee! How many people have got the nerve to do this? But because so few people bill an invoice after a meal it may be, from a business point of view, a very cheap way of getting a couple of hours of expert advice; really cheap consultancy!

A second advantage of a meal is the possibility of disclosing to others one's values, wealth and gastronomic discernment. Choosing the wine or indeed preferring mineral water to alcohol can be a clear statement about sophistication, concern about health, and preference for sobriety. Similarly, knowing one's way around a menu — a command of kitchen French and/or Italian; a familiarity with a long wine list — is a sure way of disclosing information about wealth, training and education. Being able to discuss the benefits of north-facing slopes on the softness of a Medoc or why a particular year was so poor for Bordalino may just provide the right amount of sophisticated small talk to impress a client.

Choosing health foods, being a vegetarian, or insisting on Perrier are clear indications of values and life-styles. Margaret Thatcher demanded still Malvern or Ashbourne Water in cabinet, it being more patriotic that more well-known French brands. Being a teetotaller may be a distinct disadvantage, as may being a fastidious vegetarian, as it may embarrass or restrict a host who clearly enjoys over-indulging.

How one pays the bill may also provide an excellent opportunity to show off. An ostentatious proffering of a platinum American Express card is a clear statement about one's wealth. On the other hand calling for a copy of the bill makes it far too apparent that one is not actually paying oneself and hence demonstrating largesse.

But perhaps more than any other reason it is for the ambience and conviviality that people choose to negotiate over a meal. Sometimes a lunch is a simple if not impressive bribe — hence it is never free. The reciprocity norm, upon which the whole Christmas card industry is based, demands that one pay back and not necessarily in kind, for a meal. It is a form of the great ritual of giving — the way in which paying for the meal may be a culturally approved way of establishing order and power between people of different ranks. A free lunch may be returning or paying a favour or more likely putting you in debt for a future occasion.

Business negotiation is frequently a matter of reciprocal concessions. A meal is all about reciprocity — passing the salt, pouring the wine. Furthermore if one is lost as to how to support a flagging conversation one can always introduce the subject of eating. Also talking about trivial matters can take up a large proportion of the time, no doubt because we all know more about them than important matters.

Also at luncheon meetings the only unmatched asset is the ability to yawn with one's mouth closed. They can be very boring because they are often used as occasions to sound out people when one is not quite sure how to proceed. They are deliberately agendaless and rambling.

Wine may make people indiscreet: in vino veritas. On the other hand, the lunch may be a rather good place to impart bad news. The results of a performance review or an annual appraisal can be softened by a glass or two of wine and a medicinal brandy. Some people are told that their employers feel that they can 'let them go' after they have been extravagantly fed and watered. At lunch, perhaps more than anywhere else, hypocrisy is the baseline of social intercourse. The fine food and good wine may however cloud one's judgement. After all, if one can tell the difference between good and bad advice one doesn't really need advice at all. Getting sozzled in the middle of the day can be dangerous. It is interesting that two pejorative phrases — 'Out to lunch' and 'A legend in his own lunchtime' — both hint at some of the pitfalls of the business meal. One can too easily sign a deal over the port, omitting to remember that often what the large print giveth, the small print taketh away. Of course one great way to overcome the post-luncheon 'dips' is not to stop for lunch. Order another bottle of Chablis (after all, the client/ company is paying) and keep talking till the sun goes down. Make a day of it ... and have a business dinner as well!

> ➤ There are good reasons to do business over a meal: it ensures longer working hours, and it allows one to disclose very important aspects of one's taste, wealth etc.

> ➤ Beware the motives of the business luncheon host. He or she might be getting valuable consultancy for the price of a modest meal. Beware too of letting the alcohol and atmosphere lull one into a false sense of security and letting slip relevant information.

> ➤ But use the business lunch yourself, or indeed any meal, to help your business along. It can be very cost effective.

B. Business Cards

A business card gives an executive's name, address and job title. It is an ideal way to show off.

But this business of job titles and descriptions is important, even strike-worthy, stuff. A job, at least what it is called, gives one in large measure status, identity, and respect in society at large. One of the many hardships of unemployment is that people lose their identity because one is not only what one eats, but also what one does. And so it is with retirement. A sagacious college professor who was bribed into early retirement seemed particularly concerned over what may seem to some a very trivial matter — what job title to put in his passport. After some reflection he came up with consultant — a nice ambiguous, high status title signifying essentially nothing. Like the term designer which can be placed as a prefix of any manufactured object, all of which have been designed so as to increase outrageously the price, so 'consultant' acts as convenient suffix to any job description, however humdrum, to give it status.

That no doubt is why 'real' engineers get so upset when people like street cleaners hijack that term to become sanitary engineers; dubious double-glazing salesmen become insulation engineers and furniture removers become transference engineers. Examples of this are legion and frequently pathetic, in that one witnesses many people's vain attempts to upgrade their jobs and themselves by changing the title. A bit like the re- (as opposed to the more common) de-valuing of a currency which remains the same but is somehow worth more. Unions fight over these things. One chief technician lamenting his new title that the Union had fought for no doubt in some important job re-description by differential negotiation, he was to be known as head laboratory steward, a term he quite rightly loathed. He said he felt like a second-class waiter employed to feed rats or give scientists a regular gin-and-tonic rather than a skilled and flexible electronic technician.

Job titles are important inside organizations because they are the symbol of status, power and salary, but equally important, if not more so, for dealing with people outside the organization. That is, for those who speak mid-Atlantic management-babble, career descriptions are important from an inter- and intra-organization perspective! People like to know who they are dealing with and how far up they are on the pyramidal organization. Perhaps that is why the armed forces give people honorary ranks — a clergyman is a captain, a psychologist a colonel — so that they (the inflexible military) know how to treat them properly — for instance, which mess to go to, how much to pay them, who salutes whom.

A very clever way to disclose one's job title is in business cards, those useful pieces of firm paper upon which one scribbles directions, shopping lists and addresses and which one occasionally swaps with other people in the field. Many businessmen and women have albums of these cards which are convenient ways of sorting and displaying business cards when the number mounts up, literally into hundreds. They are a bit like those once so popular cigarette cards obsessionally hoarded by avaricious collectors and pasted into great books, each one in its correct place. What would a third world anthropologist make of these cards — not quite letters of introduction or gifts. What is their function and why are they so subtly different?

Debrett's, that reputed doyen of good taste, is very specific about cards which they maintain should be engraved, not printed, on good quality paper. They distinguish between professional and business cards but they follow the same format. The 'correct' size is 3 inches by 1 inch; the name should be in the middle (followed by degrees) with the address in the bottom left-hand corner and the telephone number in the bottom right-hand corner.

But breaking the rules can be a very useful way of disclosing information about oneself. The size, colour, type-face, indeed the language, can be effectively varied. It appears that there is a curious, implicit language of business cards. Simple minimalistic black embossed on white is high status professional. The bigger the more vulgar as a rule. Creativity is disclosed by the use of colours (pastel shades) and/or the use of 'writing' as opposed to print. Some creative people alter the shape of the card to make it stand out. One should use a full name or initial but never shortened names like Chris, Bob or Chuck. The American's middle initial (Wilber P. Green) seems ubiquitous and acceptable as is trans-Atlantic spelling. One's rank or status is obligatory, such as financial Controller (Europe), Sales Manager or Executive Director, which is of course a mine-field of synonyms, euphemisms and bunkum. What is a 'Waste Management Consultant' (perhaps a free-lance dustman) and a 'Customised Entertainment Director' (an up-market whore)? Degrees, memberships and affiliations may be produced if impressive. No B.A. (Bombay), B.Com (Middle Idaho State College) or MBIM. A simple MBA, PhD or FRS is sufficient, preferably with a classy (Harvard) or (Oxon) attached. Logos are acceptable if discreet in size and colour.

One should never overdo it. It is apparently in poor taste to have daytime and evening telephone numbers — that's desperate. One should not have the obverse printed in Japanese, however impressive the implications. If one does business in Japan one should have cards printed especially for them. Some cards contain only the name so that the giver can add the information that he or she wishes — business address, home telephone number etc.

Clearly it's important to play your cards right. Sending the wrong message through the ritualized handing over of one's identity to business clients may in extreme cases lead to the deal collapsing like a house of cards!

➤ To a large extent working people's identity and self-respect is wrapped up in their jobs particulary their grade or title.

➤ While organizations differ considerably in the number and meaning attached to title (supervisors, superintendent, controller, president, director) they are very important to people within the organization.

➤ Self-employed people boost their status by impressive meaningless titles aimed to obfuscate and impress. Remember that some organisations offer impressive job titles in place of real salary.

➤ A business card is an artefact of business culture. It can say a great deal about the needs and insecurities of individuals and the structure of organizations as a whole.

C. Business Bric-a-brac

Businessmen, like traffic wardens or school boys, have a uniform. Britons who work for very high-powered American-owned management consultancies tell of the explicit rules of the company which all refer to dress. Men may only wear dark blue or grey suits; only failures wear brown. Shirts must be plain white and definitely not coloured or striped. You may express some individuality in a neck tie, but it has to be of a fashionable width, preferably with red, never loud. Women, too, have to follow rules that state in essence that the more one looks like a BA airline hostess (blue suit, court shoes, tied bow) the more appropriately one is dressed. Power dressing is still in, say the magazines, even if a little softened.

These dress rules fulfil a number of functions — they express corporate culture (serious-minded, well-prepared, conservativeness) and make the often ludicrously young consultants look older than they are. Consider the photocopy repair man trying to present the same image by arriving in a dark suit, with a large plastic briefcase which is actually a tool-box. The smooth, executive image is soon exploded as they rapidly remove their outfits, often to reveal short-sleeved (and hence cuff-link-less) shirts and rather grubby arms, as they get down to the work of repairing the machines. Shoulder pads make one seem bigger and more powerful than one is; striped clothes can help give the impression one is slimmer.

Sociologists, and others interested in organizational or corporate behaviour, have observed and studied companies in much the same way as anthropologists do with their exotic and primitive tribes. They attempt to understand the nature, function and symbolic meaning of dress, rituals and meetings, showing how some are adaptive and others not. New technology hailed the introduction of a new business fashion. The size and type of PC slung over the shoulder is clearly a statement of power. And this is most clearly expressed in the type of executive desks and briefcases now seen among the smart set.

There used to be a time when there was a positive association between one's power and status in an organization, and the size of one's desk. One still sees cartoons of dictatorial, merchant-baron, captains of industry seated behind half an acre of polished oak, glaring at a clearly intimidated employee. The desk would be relatively bare, except for assorted and expensive executive toys and trinkets (elaborate golf-club shaped clocks, gold paper-clip containers), but might also contain a selection of multicoloured phones (more equals better).

186

The imagery is clear: size is equated with power. But more importantly there would be drawers, trays, files and various other clever little niches to store paper and other documents. The grand old roll-top desks with a veritable bank of storage compartments were the best example of the genre. Information was power. It was stored on paper in files. The more of these documents and files one had, the more powerful one was. But now desks are out and tables are in. Further, the shape and size of the table reflects a rather different image. Frequently they are circular or occasionally oval, rarely oblong, never square. They are also not over-large, having space for somewhere between four and eight people — certainly never more than ten. Often they are bare, though the room should contain a computer terminal, one (at most two) telephones, a couple of good pieces of art (never a portrait, certificates, degrees), a few comfortable chairs and a couch. Colours should preferably be light so as to heighten the effect of openness. The crucial image, it seems, is one of space, lack of clutter, indeed almost emptiness.

The briefcase — a sort of mobile office — has also undergone an interesting transformation. Consider a typology of briefcases one might notice on Paddington Station. first, there is the shabby, donnish, somewhat battered leather bag. Shapeless and scarred, it is usually large so that it can contain simultaneously books, papers, overnight clothes and perhaps even the odd sandwich. Its shapelessness is primarily due to it being stretched by odd contents (eg.,. tennis rackets, a bottle or two of claret, books and papers). Then there are those fairly large square cases — the more hideous made of plastic (or some substitute) — designed not to be flexible but to have useful compartments for felt-tipped pens, one's absolutely essential Time-manager or filofax (a ridiculously over-priced diary). Thirdly, there is the 'expensive material' case that follows no shape rule except that it is made out of crocodile, calf-leather or some other unfortunate animal. Each of these cases may have monograms or initials and/or lock, both of which are, or rather were, a modest sign of status.

The modern fashion, however, is distinguished not so much by its shape or material but its size. Capable of carrying only the financial Times, the new wafer-thin briefcase is distinguished by not looking like a briefcase at all. The less one can carry in the case, the better. An unusual handle or being made out of an unusual, rare (and of course very expensive) material are essential features, but initials, locks, etc. are out.

Why have the large desk and the solid briefcase been replaced by the designer table and briefcase as thin as a folder? The answer probably lies partly in the way in which we now use, store and access information. The higher one rises within an organization, the more one becomes a pure administrator. Generals don't fight, managing directors don't deal with customers ... they all administer in the sense that they are decision makers.

They sit at meetings — that waste hours and take minutes — calling together experts, division heads or other leaders of units in their organization — the people at the top of those interesting 'organogram' flow charts of who's who in an organization. These experts have been briefed by their underlings. Each in turn has to condense information about sales, grants, movements, etc., from vast print-outs into pretty (preferably coloured) computer graphics of pie charts, histograms etc. ... a sort of visual image for the hard of thinking. The higher one is in the organization the more interpretation and selection of the data is required and the more it is boiled down. It is said old hop along Reagan refused to consider anything that could not be summarized on an A4 piece of paper.

Around the conference table, then, the decision-maker may call for information about a particular issue. This information has no doubt been carried to the meeting by the lieutenant in a briefcase, slightly bigger than that of the person above him. And his briefing has already occurred at various levels, each time with an underling providing more and more material and print-outs that the person above him or her selects, edits and precis and so reduces in size. Thus, just as with the porters of David Livingstone and Edmund Hilary, the more one carries the lowlier one is.

One should, it seems, aim to travel light and, despite the warning of Aneurin Bevan in another context, 'go naked into the conference chamber'.

➤ The clue to a person's power and rank can be seen in manifold items — clothes, office, desk, briefcase.

➤ The particular characteristics of each item may change along with changes in technology and the way business is done.

➤ But to be an effective communicator in any organization one needs to read the messages. Business attire and furnishings are not based purely on personal taste and preference. They represent the language of power.

CONCLUSION

Seventh Heaven: Ways of Growing Rich

Success stories of business superstars are certainly as interesting and improbable as the biographies of minor European monarchs or film stars. Many tycoons can tell the 'tea-boy-to-Managing Director' fable of how they made it from humble beginnings to multi-million-dollar moguls. Many of these tales are of an occasionally moving roller-coaster ride through early success, false starts and repeated failure, with the only comparison on this lonely journey being a consistent motivation to succeed.

But by definition, these auto-hagiographies are the enviable stories of success. How people become rich is the stuff of dreams; the hope of every lottery ticket buyer and the fantasy of every gambler. Most people have imagined what they would do if they won the pools. But no self-made billionaires are such idle time wasters. They have all worked hard for long periods to find those extremely elusive secrets of success that lead to mega-riches. They are proponents of the adage that 'success' comes before 'work' only in the dictionary.

The so-called secrets are of course often well known. People who have studied the histories of business achievement have in fact documented various possible routes to the same end: the sweet but distinctive smell of success. A careful examination of the major pathways to company growth has revealed how relatively few they are in number. Case studies have shown for instance that the success of companies like Walt Disney, Benetton, Korean Airlines, Federal Express, Hilton Hotels, Gucci and the Mandarin Hotel group was achieved via different pathways.

Business School researchers like Simon Tam, at Hong Kong University Business School, have argued that in fact there are only really seven distinct routes to significant business success. All hyper-growth firms surveyed appear to fit into one or other of these seven categories. All companies following one pathway might experience the same benefits, but they also share the same vulnerabilities. The seven routes are distinct though they may exist in various combinations within large groups or overtime. They are:

1 **The Product Innovation Route:** Here the business is built on one or more extremely successful, original and unique products. Polaroid is such an example and so is Sony. Products may be as varied as instant noodles to adult magazines, but their companies succeed, after a long search, researching the unique, innovative and, of course, highly desirable new product.

2   The Technological Innovation Route: Here business success lies not in finding a new product, but rather a new way of producing it. Honda added an engine to a bicycle, and Evergreen thought of container ships. Many have, sometimes through luck, discovered a new way to do things. And they have become extremely rich in doing so.

3   The Relationship Route: All business people know about contacts and networking, but few make it the secret of their success. Rothschild, Khashoggi and Hammer all got rich by establishing and maintaining highly beneficial relationships with politicians, the military, corporations and royalty. They certainly believed that God gave us our friends and the Devil our relations.

4   Exploiting the Rigid Competitor Route: Some firms have succeeded by spotting not a gap in the market, but the lazy, inflexible, rigid competitor. Regulatory change and the opening of legal loopholes means that some entrepreneurs have anticipated and used the opportunity. Freddie Laker, Federal Express and DHL typify those who made their killing by exploiting the complacency of others.

5   Turnaround Route: Some have made it rich by a dramatic and unpredicted turnaround of poorly functioning companies. Individuals have taken weakly functioning organizations and changed then into vigorous, customer-sensitive, dollar-generating companies. Hilton Hotels and first Pacific nicely illustrate this route.

6   The Market Forces Route: Some people are, it seems, super-sensitive to consumers' psychology. Those with the metaphorical ears on the railway line of market forces have included Gucci, Saatchi and Saatchi and Lotte. These highly successful businessmen have successfully capitalized, mobilized and manipulated market forces to their own ends.

7   The Exceptional Service Route: There are those, like Singapore Airlines and the Mandarin Hotel chain, whose success is almost entirely attributable to going beyond currently conceivable levels of service. The potential customer becomes a regular customer and a happy free advertiser by word of mouth for the company. It's hard work but such companies are proof that it can be done and there are rich pickings once the reputation for service has been won and the prices can be marked.

The problem with all lists or category systems is that the hair-splitter finds unclassifiable or combination routes. Others, hoping for eponymous fame, devise alternative classification systems.

But rather than figure out a perfect and parsimonious nomenclature for becoming rich, it may be better to begin the journey.